Praise for

HOW FAR TO THE PROMISED LAND

"In these pages are words that redeem time and refresh the human spirit. . . . The timeliness of Esau McCaulley's honest, hope-filled story—told with depth, precision, and purpose—feels like a balm for the weary soul."

—Charlie Dates, senior pastor of
Salem Baptist and Progressive Baptist

"As soon as I finished, I wanted to reread. McCaulley is already recognized as a great scholar and essayist, but this is his best writing yet. The storytelling here is both poetic and prophetic, free of both superficiality and cynicism. Read this book and the words will linger with you."

—Russell Moore, editor in chief of *Christianity Today*

"McCaulley gives his readers an offering to peer into the window of his soul and that of his southern Black family. It is a story of the convergence of structural racism and the grace of God, which carries them on as they traverse the rugged terrain of life to the promised land."

—Ekemini Uwan, public theologian and NAACP
Image Award–nominated co-author of *Truth's Table*

"A thoughtfully written book that offers heartfelt, empathetic lessons without preaching to the choir."

—*Kirkus Reviews*

"Powerful . . . McCaulley uses examples of his own family's stories of survival over time to remind readers that some paths to the promised land have detours along the way."

—*The Root,* Books by Black Authors
We Can't Wait to Read

"Esau McCaulley's riveting memoir holds together tensions that many of us pry apart: systemic injustice and personal responsibility, accountability and forgiveness, honesty and sympathy. This book is prophetic without being preachy, and heartwarming without being cloying. . . . A triumph of storytelling."

—Tish Harrison Warren, author of
Liturgy of the Ordinary

"With uncompromising honesty and deep introspection, McCaulley complicates the narrative of 'overcoming racism and poverty as a hero.' . . . Powerful and necessary."

—*Publishers Weekly* (starred review)

HOW FAR TO THE PROMISED LAND

HOW FAR
=== TO THE ===
PROMISED LAND

*One Black Family's Story of Hope
and Survival in the American South*

ESAU MCCAULLEY

CONVERGENT
NEW YORK

Published in the United States by Convergent Books,
an imprint of Random House, a division of
Penguin Random House LLC, New York.

CONVERGENT BOOKS is a registered trademark and the Convergent colophon is a trademark of Penguin Random House LLC.

Originally published in hardcover in the United States
by Convergent Books, an imprint of Random House, a division of Penguin
Random House LLC, in 2023.

LIBRARY OF CONGRESS CATALOGING-IN-PUBLICATION DATA
Names: McCaulley, Esau, author.
Title: How far to the promised land / by Esau McCaulley.
Description: First edition. | New York: Convergent Books, [2023]
Identifiers: LCCN 2023011990 (print) | LCCN 2023011991 (ebook) |
ISBN 9780593241103 (trade paperback) | ISBN 9780593241097 (ebook)
Subjects: LCSH: McCaulley, Esau—Childhood and youth. |
McCaulley, Esau, Sr., 1960–2017—Family. | McCaulley family. |
African American families—Alabama—Social conditions. |
African Americans—Alabama—Huntsville—Social conditions. |
Poor Black people—Alabama—Biography. |
Huntsville (Ala.)—Biography.
Classification: LCC E185.93.A3 M33 2023 (print) | LCC E185.93.A3 (ebook) |
DDC 305.5/6908996073092 [B]—dc23/eng/20230512
LC record available at https://lccn.loc.gov/2023011990
LC ebook record available at https://lccn.loc.gov/2023011991

Printed in the United States of America on acid-free paper

convergentbooks.com

1st Printing

This book is dedicated to my mother, Laurie McCaulley.
Whatever else I am, I will always remain your son.

He also told this parable to some who trusted in themselves that they were righteous and regarded others with contempt: "Two men went up to the temple to pray, one a Pharisee and the other a tax collector. The Pharisee, standing by himself, was praying thus, 'God, I thank you that I am not like other people: thieves, rogues, adulterers, or even like this tax collector. I fast twice a week; I give a tenth of all my income.' But the tax collector, standing far off, would not even look up to heaven, but was beating his breast and saying, 'God, be merciful to me, a sinner!'"

—LUKE 18:9–13

Contents

Black Narratives and American Dreams

I n March 2019, I agreed, after much hesitation, to join a panel at the University of North Carolina. Having committed to a speaking engagement in Tennessee the following evening, I'd initially demurred. But in a last-ditch effort to convince me to come, the organizer informed me that the Grammy Award–winning recording artist Lecrae would be the other speaker and panelist. Providence was with him, because the date coincided with the birthday of my oldest son, Luke, and Lecrae happened to be one of Luke's favorite hip-hop artists. How could I resist?

Luke beamed when I told him the plan. He picked out his favorite New England Patriots hoodie for the journey and told all his friends at school, treating two days of one-on-one time with his father as the rarity that it was. Seeing him prepare brought to mind an ill-fated road trip with my father that happened when I was around the same age. But I forced that memory to the back of my mind and focused on the present, allowing my son's excitement to overcome the beginnings of melancholy. I noted that he'd remembered to pack his asthma medicine, changes of clothing, and even a pack of gum, to keep his ears from popping on the flight.

The next day, a friendly volunteer met us at the airport and drove us to campus for a tour. Having left behind the forty-degree chill typical of early spring in Rochester, we enjoyed a warm and breezy walk among the sights and sounds of Chapel Hill. Our student host chatted with Luke, seeming more interested in this youth with a mini Afro and articulately stated preadolescent opinions than the scholar come to town.

Still, despite the pleasant welcome, a campus visit to discuss anti-Black racism carries the tension inherent in any discussion of race. I'd been invited to show that Christianity can be a friend, rather than a foe, of social justice by addressing how faith helps us resolve what W.E.B. Du Bois famously called "the problem of the color line"—this to a college still reeling from a series of protests in 2018 that climaxed with the tearing down of a Confederate statue on university grounds. Speaking at these events, I sometimes feel like a doctor telling a patient that their illness is more serious than first thought. Recovery will not simply involve taking medication; it must include surgery and a change in lifestyle. The truth stings, making hostility toward the bearer of such bad news inevitable.

As I took to the stage alongside our host and Lecrae, I looked out at the audience—a gathering of earnest-looking white students with a sprinkling of chocolate bodies. I saw in their posture and stares a familiar mixture of skepticism and hope. I knew what the Black students were thinking: *What will he say? Is he here to speak about Black people or to us? Will he tell the truth or curry favor to keep his role as appointed representative of the race?* I sat in similar auditoriums as an undergrad, my head stuffed with the writings of James Baldwin, Zora Neale Hurston, Martin Luther King, Jr., and a multitude of Bible verses. Part of me longed for those days, when it was easy to imagine that my words and writings would one day prove the truth of anti-Black racism and move people to resist its effects on society. But I was no longer in the audience, nor had I been for quite some time. I felt less sure of myself. Racism persists for a reason, and experience had taught me that change is not the work of one speech or book.

Nonetheless, I did what was asked of me. I tried to bring the teachings of Christianity and my knowledge of Black history, literature, and the African American church to bear on the evening's topic. As the night wore on, my words seemed to have some effect. Audience members who'd started the evening pinned to the backs of their seats now leaned forward. The crowd began to respond with applause. My energy was good, no doubt spurred on by the opportunity to make Luke proud. I could see him sitting with a group of college students in the front row, the youngest face among a sea of emerging adults.

The Q&As that follow such talks are always tricky. You never know what questions or paradoxes audience members might have for you. To keep the conversation on track, the questions had been screened beforehand. I knew the drill, but toward the end of our time together, it was the host who asked something that stumped me: "To help our audience, please tell us about one of the most racist things you have experienced."

The request was framed as a way of drawing the audience in. Maybe the questioner thought a dose of pathos was needed to drive home the point that racism is wicked. Still, as a Black man speaking to a mostly white audience, I winced. I answered before my fellow panelist had a chance to respond: "Can we pass on that one? We'll pass."

Until recently, I would have dutifully complied. On stages and in print, I would cut myself open and bleed in hopes that my pain and suffering would help bring justice to my people. It was how I'd been taught to speak. I recall meeting with my guidance counselor near the end of high school and asking, "How do I fill out these college applications? What should I put in my scholarship essay?" What I meant was *How do I please these white people who have my future in their hands when they've never been in my neighborhood, never stepped into my school, never traveled the streets of Huntsville, Alabama, in this dark flesh that is often viewed with suspicion?* My counselor, long experienced in such matters, told me to write about all the obstacles I'd faced. "Tell them your story and the things you overcame. Make them feel the difference that letting you into the school will make in your life." Colleges, she explained, wanted to know they had the opportunity to pluck a branch from the burning fires of poverty before it was consumed.

So I learned to tell the story America requires from its

Black survivors. I wrote about overcoming an absent, drug-addicted father, anti-Black racism, and childhood poverty to earn a high school diploma and a shot at higher education. In that version of events, my father and the people I encountered along the way became cautionary tales, the tragic backdrop to my feats of grit and determination. It worked. Despite having adequate but not exceptional grades, I was accepted at a nationally ranked college with generous financial aid; from there I went on to seminary, graduate school, and a career as a university professor and columnist.

The moderator's request carried a predetermined plot. By revealing a horrific experience I had survived, by relating how I had become a more determined person for it, I would be rewarded with the audience's sympathy, just as I had won over the sympathy of the college admissions committees decades earlier.

But that night, onstage, I realized that something had shifted. I did not want to speak about overcoming racism and poverty as a hero. Nobody escapes poverty; we are marked by it. The friends, relationships, and traumas we experienced linger. We carry them wherever we go.

And the spotlight in these narratives is too narrow. A good narrative—a Black one, at least—is not owned by any individual; it is, instead, the story of a people. The focus on a singular person obscures the truth that the gifted are not the only ones who succeed, the weak are not the only ones who perish, and the America we laud for producing victors still creates too many victims to be at ease with the way things are. Instead of hearing about the worst hardship I had experienced, what the audience needed was for me to talk about the community and the family that shaped me—the people normally written out of such stories—and how the struggle in each life to find meaning and purpose, regardless of its outcome, has a chance to teach us what it means to be human.

In the end, my declining to answer is what this book is about. What I owed the audience, yes, but my people first and foremost. A story not about *me* but about *us*.

My desire to tell my story in a different and truer way had begun two years earlier. On the night of August 26, 2017, my father, Esau McCaulley, Sr., died unexpectedly. I was thirty-seven years old and married to a woman I had met in college. Mandy and I had four kids—two boys and two girls—ranging in age from nine to one. We lived in a four-bedroom house in Rochester, New York, that could fit the four houses of my childhood inside it.

In our Rochester neighborhood, there were no sirens or shouts from feuding couples next door. There was no momentary pause while the neighbors held their breath, deciding whether the loud noise they'd just heard came from a gunshot or a car backfiring. It seemed fitting that the neighborhood was known as Park Ave, bringing to mind one of the highest-valued properties on the Monopoly board. Its tree-lined blocks were filled with old Victorians, Craftsman homes, and colonials of every color, many with sweeping porches that made it easy to greet neighbors as they walked their dogs on the well-manicured sidewalks. Our house was precious to me, a red-and-green Victorian built in 1888. Moving into that home felt like an arrival of sorts, the last step on my journey to the promised land.

That night, the phone woke me from a deep sleep, its ring reminding me of the ten years I had worked as a pastor. Almost every evening back then, my phone would buzz with news of an illness or a family turmoil, and I would rush out to visit the hospital or counsel a married couple in crisis. As a clergyperson, my goal was to be available to my parishioners, never to let down someone in need. But since I'd slipped into my new role as a professor, my phone no longer rang past midnight. I knew the news was bad even before I answered.

It was my older sister, Latasha. I could tell from the sound of her voice that she'd been weeping, but as a pediatrician who oversaw an intensive care unit, she was used to delivering difficult news to grieving family members. She cleared her throat. "Dad died in California. His truck veered off an overpass and fell onto the highway below. No other cars were involved. We do not know what caused him to do that yet."

With the news now delivered, Latasha became my sister again, and she wept. But the truth of her words had not yet reached me. I did not cry. I felt empty, like when you finish a meal still hungry.

A decade prior, I might have said something callous or trite. The man who had caused us so much pain was dead. Now I did not know what to say. "Thank you for telling me," I said, withdrawing into formality.

Mandy had woken up and sat beside me, her concern showing in the delicate set of wrinkles that framed her eyes.

I thought about how much I loved those little lines, earned from a lifetime of fretting over the coughs and sniffles of young patients and the bumps and bruises our children managed to collect. "Are you okay?" she asked once I'd hung up.

I told her I didn't know, and I dialed my mother. She was crying, too. Next came my younger sister, Marketha, and my brother, Brandon. Eventually all five of us found ourselves on a group call, sharing light stories about my father and avoiding the heavy ones as best we could.

Once that call had ended, I lay back down in bed, but sleep eluded me. I was anticipating the conversation that would come the next day. My family would need to plan a funeral, and a funeral required a eulogy. I ran through two options: The Reverend Theodore Bone was my mother's father. He was the natural choice, as the family patriarch and a respected clergyperson in the part of Alabama where I'd grown up. But after opposing my parents' relationship from the beginning, he'd never gotten to know my father very well—and what little he knew, he didn't like. There was also the pastor of my childhood church, the Reverend Oscar Montgomery, but my father had not attended church with us.

That night, lying in the dark, I understood as certainly as I knew that the sun would rise that my father's eulogy would need to be delivered by me. Like the Reverends Bone and Montgomery, I was a clergyperson, but unlike them, I shared a name with my father and, at times, had shared a home— although much of that period had been fraught and worrisome. Still, I did not know the details of his life well. Our in-depth conversations had been few and far between, curtailed by what little a young child and a father on drugs have to say to each other.

The next afternoon, I called my mother again. Southern standards of decorum required us to pretend that something other than death was on our minds. "How are the kids?" she asked. "Are you enjoying life as a professor?" When I got around to asking about the funeral, she told me it might need to be delayed by a few weeks because a spate of murders in Bakersfield over the weekend left ten bodies to be autopsied ahead of my father's.

Steeling myself, I told my mother what I'd been thinking: "I believe that I should do the eulogy."

"We agree," she said, not hesitating for a second. "Your sister Marketha called me earlier and said, 'I don't want nobody speaking about our daddy except my big brother. He is the only one that will tell the truth.'"

Then my mother paused, thinking it over one last time. "Are you sure you can do it?"

I replied, "I'm not sure I have a choice."

I knew this work. As a clergyperson, I had delivered eulogies before. I understood that the pastor's job is to find meaning in unfinished lives. Because few people have the opportunity to set their affairs in order and make amends for all the things gone wrong, it becomes the job of the clergy to provide closure for grieving friends and relatives. Anyone close to the deceased can tell a fond story about them, but clergy are tasked with something deeper: connecting the life of the deceased to the wider purposes of God.

Even before I began, part of me understood that asking

the question of who my father was would involve coming to accept the role he'd played—good and bad—in making me who I am. His story and mine are not so easily separated. It had taken me most of my life to begin the process of forgiving him. I had set off down that path, but I had not yet learned to regard him with much tenderness. To eulogize him, I would need to see him clearly, as someone whose story deserved to be treated with care.

My father's death ushered in a season of truth telling. I would begin to let my children in on the story of their grandfather and their ancestors before him—stories I have collected here. I would tell them about my own childhood, about growing up poor, about meeting their mother, and the struggles we had in making a life together. In telling those family stories, I would begin to teach them about America, its past misdeeds and triumphs. I would make more of myself known to them.

In the end, I would tell my kids that we, the McCaulleys, are a people born of trauma and miracle. By that, I mean we have experienced the traumas American society has inflicted upon Black people for centuries *and* the harm we've done to ourselves. We come from a long line of wanderers, looking this way and that, trying to find the promised land in a country that has never loved Black people well. Nonetheless, when tragedy—fire, disease, sickness, and physical violence—has threatened to undo us entirely, God has intervened and performed miracles. By miracle, I do not mean a simple rescue, an escape from danger. Instead, like the ancient Israelites finding their way in the desert, we have received just enough manna in the wilderness to make it to another day.

HOW FAR TO THE PROMISED LAND

Part I

ABSENCE AND PRESENCE

CHAPTER 1

The Making of a Villain

My father and mother met in the winter of 1976. I've seen photos, stored in a box in the utility closet next to the washing machine and a mop better suited for spreading water around than clearing grime off floors. In these photos, my parents' clothes are more a battle for supremacy between pastels than anything resembling coherent outfits. There they are, looking as young and untroubled as any two high school students on a Friday night date. Not yet parents, not weighed down with the responsibility of caring for four children, both are smiling, my father standing behind my mother, who sits on a stool with her head nestled into his chest.

They met not long after the Jim Crow laws were replaced by practices more subtle and harder to combat. Segregation was technically outlawed, but custom divided my mother's hometown of Huntsville into sections. "Things were pretty separated in Huntsville," my mom recalls. "I cannot remember one time when we partied together. We had Black house parties and white ones, even among students in integrated schools."

The Parkway Place mall demarcated the white part of town. Located at the intersection of Drake Avenue and Memorial Parkway, it was close enough to the Black section of Huntsville for my mom to feel comfortable visiting. Another mall, called Heart of Huntsville, located deeper into the white area, seemed off-limits. My mother remembers security following her from the time she walked in until she exited: "One security guard for every Black person they saw."

My parents were introduced by my father's cousin Larry, whose easy smile and welcoming personality marked him as a charmer. Larry and my mom attended school at J. O. Johnson High, where he was two years ahead of her. Intrigued by the sly older boy, my mother dated him, but after the second outing, she opted to let him down easy by introducing him to her friend Wanda. Larry, in turn, suggested that my mother meet his cousin Esau, who went to school out in the country, at Gurley High.

On that first date, my mother is instantly drawn to my father's tenderness. She will come to know him as outgoing and funny, but tonight he acts shy and polite. It's the 1970s, and, playing to the stereotype of the decade as I imagine it, they spend the evening parked at a drive-in movie. In the front seat, Larry and Wanda are hitting it off. Encouraged by his prospects, Larry turns to Esau and says, "Go ahead, cousin, lean in and give her a kiss."

My dad will have none of it. "I just met the girl," he says. "I ain't kissing nothing."

After the date, my mom boasts that my dad was "the perfect gentleman." She does not yet know that his tenderness comes from grief, which lingers at the edge of his attempts at humor and charm. After a few dates, in a real show of vulnerability, he tells her, "My father died a few months back. Right before he died, he told my mother that my brother Barney and I weren't no good. I just thought that I would give you fair warning."

Believing she can fix what is broken, my mother is hooked. When I prodded her for information years later, she told me, "I think that his whole life he was trying to prove a dead man wrong."

My dad was six feet tall, with an athletic build from his time as a basketball player, his brown skin a shade lighter than the ebony complexion I inherited from farther up the family tree. His Afro was medium-sized and tasteful, such that it both fit with the natural style of the time and could be maintained at the same length without drawing much attention in the 1980s and 1990s. He didn't have the most expensive clothes, but they were always clean and well ironed. That tendency for cleanliness would remain his whole life. According to my mom, he was "fine as the day is long, and all the girls wanted him."

After they had dated for a short time, my father, Esau Sr., brought his new girl home to meet his mother, Wavon, and his grandmother Sophia. According to my mother, Sophia took one look at her and opined, "That is a very good woman right there. You don't deserve her, Esau." Turning to my mother, she said, "Laurie Ann, you seem like a nice girl. I would run. This boy will be the source of unending trials for you." Used to barbs like this, my father didn't defend himself. His normally wide smile tightened, and he lowered his gaze.

My mother did not know how to process Sophia's warning. Even now, she is not clear on whether she should have heeded it. When pressed, she returns to the fact that the relationship that gave her so much pain also produced four cherished children.

She made her decision about the man who would shape the rest of her life at Johnson High School, between the ages of sixteen and eighteen. They were just kids, and their courtship was brief. By the spring of 1977, my mother's junior year, she was pregnant with my sister Latasha. They married in the summer of 1979, six months before my birth. My mother is not yet showing in the wedding pictures, but I am there, forming in her belly, when they exchange their vows and first kiss as a married couple.

Once they married, my parents moved into a trailer on the land where my father grew up. My great-grandmother Sophia and grandmother Wavon still lived together in the larger house to the right of the gravel road that divided the plot in two. After a few years, when my folks had saved enough money to afford a place of their own, they rented a tiny three-bedroom house in a lower-class neighborhood near Alabama A&M University, the historically Black college in our city, a neighborhood for people who were broke but not yet on government assistance.

I was excited to get out of the trailer and move into the city. The well water on Grandma's property always tasted funny. With few kids my age to play with, I spent much of my time watching TV, learning about what happens to people who live in a single-wide from news reports about trailers being swept up by tornadoes every spring. Our new home would be built into the ground, not balanced uneasily on top of cinder blocks.

The new house doesn't have much furniture when we move in. That first night, my father brings home McDonald's, which we eat sitting on the kitchen floor under light cast from our only lampstand. Brandon, my little brother, still a toddler, contents himself with Gerber, a family staple. The light is dingy, but we sit together smiling and talking.

That night, I have not experienced enough of life to realize that happiness will not continue indefinitely. Instead, I figure we will gather regularly for family meals. We will become the Huxtables from *The Cosby Show* or the Seavers from *Growing Pains*. We might not have a deluxe apartment in the sky like the Jeffersons, but we no longer live in a home that has wheels. My fond memory of that night may explain why, whenever I'm restless, stressed, or sad, I like to scroll through listings on real estate websites. Houses offer a chance to dream about the lives we might live inside them and the people we might become.

A little while after we move in, I begin to play sports. I am five when my father signs me up to become a member of the Lakewood Rams. Our gold jerseys match the color of the NFL franchise, but the material feels like plastic and scratches like wool. The numbers on the uniforms look like they were cut from black electrical tape. After a few washes, some jerseys are missing portions of their numbers, so that 88 begins to look more like 44.

We are, all of us, Black boys, ranging in color from high yellow to deep chocolate, and from short and chubby to tall and slender. The coaches are a hodgepodge of former athletes, none of whom made it all the way to the future in the pros that we long to see. But it doesn't matter to us. We follow their every instruction like the words that God gave Moses on Mount Sinai.

At our first practice, I learn how to get into a three-point stance. The coach blows his whistle and shouts, "Spread your legs shoulder width apart. Bend your knees. Get on the balls of your feet. Now lean forward and put one hand on the ground." Half the kids fall over.

"All right, McCaulley, you seem to be able to get into a stance. I want you to try to get past Jackson over there. He is going to try and block you. Run him over and get to the quarterback."

That being the sum total of the instruction I will receive, I look up, unsteady in my newly acquired stance, and wait for the whistle. Then I charge. I quickly learn that the coaches' goal is to figure out which of us has the stomach for the violence necessary to play a sport built on collisions. It turns out that I love the contact and embrace it from the start.

There are other skills beyond the violence. We dash around cones and plunge our feet into and out of a row of tires designed to improve our agility. The most gifted of us get to practice running with the ball, throwing, and catching. I don't get selected for those drills. The willingness to place my body in harm's way is all I have, and I offer myself up enthusiastically.

My heart is warm because when I look over to the fence that separates the parents from the field of play, I see my father smiling and cheering for me. In this moment, he is no different from the multitude of parents all over the world who show up and yell in support of their children's first halting attempts at athletics. With my dad watching, I feel like Superman. Or, better yet, my favorite X-Men character Wolverine. I can scale any wall, vanquish any foe.

When I get home, he tells my mom how well I did: "That boy's got potential. He might be something."

After dinner, he takes me out to the backyard and reviews the stance:

Spread your legs this far.

Get on the balls of your feet so that you're ready to move left or right.

No father believes that his son will be a lineman, so we play some catch as well. He warns, "Keep your eye on the ball or it will hit you in the face." I run passing routes and take handoffs from my father. I am happy. Still, life is not like it is on TV. Unlike *Family Matters*, there is no Urkel next door; Bud from *The Cosby Show* does not stop by. The only neighborly visits at our house involve my father's drinking and smoking buddies. They gather in the living room to watch TV. My father is one of the few Black NASCAR fans I will ever meet, but he can never convince the other neighborhood folks to watch it, so the channel inevitably gets switched to football. The beer flows as the games progress, and they make jokes about Dallas Cowboy cheerleaders that soar over the comprehension of my young mind.

The tentativeness I will learn to recognize in my mother's voice as she welcomes my father's friends into our house, the hesitancy in her movements as she passes around the snacks, are still some ways off. My mother is aware of my father's bad habits, but for now, they don't seem that big a deal to her. He drinks a little and smokes a little, like everyone else.

Clean, my father bursts with life. His smile spreads out from his lips, up through his cheeks, and into his eyes. His whole face radiates joy when he laughs. And he laughs often. Everyone agrees that my dad is hilarious, the kind of man who has a nickname for every family member, friend, or neighbor. When he meets you, he sizes you up and decides whether you are an Onion Head, a Potato Head, or even, occasionally, a Banana Head. Whatever he decides to call you, that's your name. The habit of renaming everyone he meets is the one practice of his that I adopt as an adult.

Shortly after my parents' wedding, my father begins working as a truck driver. It's the one job he will return to whenever the terms of his parole do not prohibit travel out of state. Maybe he is drawn to it because driving carries with it an element of escape. He can be on the road, unconstrained by the demands of family and the limits of being poor, Black, and undereducated. He can be whoever he wants to be to the other truckers he talks to on the CB radio. He can be gone for days at a time and return home a hero with money in his pocket.

When he comes back, he tells his jokes and boasts of his

exploits, and we are all so happy to see him. When it is time to leave again, I beg him to take me with him. I want to be his copilot, to travel with him on the road and have adventures. He promises that one day he will take me.

When I am eight or nine, old enough to insist, he finally relents.

I jump up and down and run over to my mom. "Did you hear? Did you hear? Dad and I are going on a road trip." My mom smiles, happy to see me happy.

I pack my bag with a few outfits, my Optimus Prime Transformer toy, and my Bible. My mom comes in to make sure that I have all the things I really need, like my asthma inhaler, a toothbrush, and enough socks and underwear. While I prepare everything, my dad chats with Latasha in the living room. She has no interest in going on the road, but she is excited to have a few days without her little brother to get on her nerves.

Rolling my bag from my bedroom to the front room, I am ready for the open road. I have never left my hometown, nor have I ever been alone with my father for longer than it takes for my mom to have a quick nap or go to the store. But I gather my courage, doing everything I can to look like I am mature enough to handle an extended trip.

Just as I'm about to head outside, he stops me. "Son, I need to run to the store and get us snacks for the trip. Then I'll come back and get you."

"Sure, Dad," I say.

While he is at the store, I review the contents of my suitcase to make sure I have everything I need. Then I go outside to wait for him. What should be a fifteen-minute jaunt starts to seem frighteningly long. Cars, delivery trucks, and the occasional SUV rumble past our home, but no eighteen-wheelers.

After an hour, my mom comes outside. She is gentle, calling me by my middle name in a silent nod to the fact that my given name, Esau, evokes too much pain. "I don't think he's coming back, Daniel."

Fighting back tears, I wipe at my eyes. "I know he'll come for me. I know it." I wait until the sun gives way, and then I wheel my bag back inside. We will not see him again for months. He does not call or check in. One day he just returns home as if nothing has happened. I never ask to travel with him again.

There is no subtle shift or slow descent. His addiction springs into my life fully formed, dividing the man in two. One man is the kind and funny person I love, the other much more formidable. My mom tells me that he switched from marijuana to the hard stuff while on the road. "His trucking buddies introduced him to crack," she remembers, "and he was never the same." The drugs turn my father into something cold and terrible, a danger to my siblings, my mother, and me.

On days as unpredictable as the lottery balls that dash the hopes of every poor person who's purchased a ticket at a gas station, he leaves the house and returns home in a rage. The slamming of the door and the barrage of profanities indicate a rough evening ahead. Inevitably, he finds fault with something my mother has done:

Why is this house so f*cking dirty all the time? Can you clean?
Why does this dinner taste like sh*t?

And you, son, I hear you acting up in school. If I hear of that again, I am going to wear your hind out. You hear me?

What's a matter? Why are you so quiet? You scared now? Why weren't you scared when you were acting a fool in that school?

When he is high, he hits us whether we answer or remain silent. There is no clear path out of danger.

Kneeling at my bed at night, I pray that God will help me grow so that I can defend my family. Too small and weak to fight back, I do what my mother has taught me to do: I cry out to God. In the Bible, Esau and Jacob are brothers. Jacob is the chosen one. It is Jacob, not Esau, who wrestles with God during the night, trying to come to grips with his calling and destiny. But within the four walls of our Huntsville home, it is Esau Jr. who tussles with the Almighty.

I know many people who have struggled to believe in a God who allows such suffering, especially of innocent children. To them, my childhood pain is evidence that God either doesn't care or isn't powerful enough to help. Religion, they then conclude, is a false promise that keeps people shackled in fear, waiting for a salvation that never arrives.

Such criticism becomes even more urgent in Black contexts, where the question of why God didn't intervene to end slavery sooner looms large. Where was God on the slave ship, in the cotton fields, in courtrooms where innocent men and women were condemned to death for crimes they did not commit? Where was God when I was a child in need of his protection? There is no Black faith that doesn't wrestle with the problem of evil.

My reply to these questions is: We who have suffered must have some say in how that suffering is interpreted. We won the right, through our scars, to discern the significance of what we endured. My grasp of that significance begins with my experiences of God as a child, on my knees in front of my twin bed, hands clasped and eyes shut tight in prayer, repeating the simplest of prayers: "Help."

In those prayers, God came to me not with logical explanations of the problem of evil but with his presence. When I prayed, a sensation of warmth that began in my chest moved throughout my body. The room seemed less empty. The lack of a speedy deliverance frustrated and perplexed me, but I never doubted my experiences of God. It was how I survived. God and I have been through hard times together; we have a relationship born of that intimacy. If there is a testimony that deserves our attention, it is the large number of folks who believe there is no other way to tell the Black story in the United States without affirming that God carried us through.

Prayer did not resolve all my issues. With my father, the difficulty was not just the abuse; I felt ashamed. I didn't want anyone to know what happened inside our home. I didn't pour my heart out to friends or teachers. But I knew they sensed that something was wrong, because the police visited my house multiple times a year.

One night—I cannot be more than eight or nine years old, because I am sleeping in the glow-in-the-dark Transformers sleeping bag I got for my birthday—I am awakened by yelling. Usually when I'm scared, I zip it all the way up and slide all the way to the bottom, making sure that no part of my body is visible. But tonight, instead of burrowing down, I unzip the bag, roused to action by the sound of something crashing in the hallway. With concern for my mother overtaking my fear, I tiptoe to the door. Upon exiting my room, I see, next to the closed door of my parents' bedroom, a hole in the wall—made, I presume, by my father's fist or leg going through it. Then I see my father's back. "Open this g*ddamned door right now, Laurie Ann. Open it!"

My mother shouts back from inside the room, "You better get outta here, Esau! I have called the police." Frustrated that he can't get in, he makes his way outside, kicking another hole in the wall as he goes and yanking the side door off its hinge. Too wrapped up in his rage to notice my presence, he walks right past me.

I pray the police will arrive soon. And they do. My mother emerges from her room with a bloodied lip and a half-ripped shirt. She adjusts her clothing and speaks in the proper English required when addressing agents of the state.

My father goes off to jail, and I return to my sleeping bag. The next morning, I get up, get dressed, and go to school. What else is there to do but carry on? I, like so many other children, bring my trauma with me to class. I sit in the back and crack jokes, because my adrenaline is still so high that I cannot pay attention to the teacher.

Those nights spent in fear set the trajectory for the rest of my life. They simplify my dreams: All I want is to love and be loved. I want to have children who go to school without shame and secrets weighing them down like book bags much too heavy for them to carry. I never want the woman I love to have hands reaching for her with affection in one moment and malice the next. My father's failures turn me into a family man at a young age.

Hate is such a simple emotion, and for long stretches of time it is all I feel. It provides me with a sense of clarity and moral superiority. I believe I have unraveled the world's great mysteries by age ten. There are good guys and bad guys. My father is the latter; I will be the former.

One night years later, my father returns home from yet another night of drinking and drugs and starts making threats to my mom and sisters. Older now, in the seventh or eighth grade, I go to the kitchen and pick up a pot and a knife. Holding the knife in one hand and the pot in the other, I tell my father, "You are not hitting anyone else in this house again." My hands tremble. I am not sure what I will do if he decides to test my resolve. Instead, he says, "F*ck you and this house," and he storms out.

Shortly after this incident, he will be arrested on a theft charge. He will cycle in and out of jail for the next few years. In his absence, my mother, my siblings, and I come into ourselves. We gain confidence. He won't be in a place to harm us again.

But his constant departures and brief returns mean that for most of my childhood, my mother and her four children—Latasha, Marketha, Brandon, and myself—go it alone in a world made to swallow up poor Black families.

You might expect that my father's departure would draw my mother closer to her parents, but it didn't. Surprisingly, she began to spend more time with my father's mother: Grandma Wavon.

Maybe it was the bond built from living on the same property at the beginning of my parents' marriage, or maybe it was because my grandmother knew what it was like to raise children alone. In any case, we returned often to see Grandma Wavon. While my siblings and I would play outside, my mother would sit in the front room, and they would chat the afternoon away.

Whenever Wavon saw me, she would call me over and say, "Old man Daniel prayed three times a day," recounting the story of my namesake from the Bible. She explained that Daniel was taken from his homeland in Israel and carried off into exile in Babylon. Despite all the temptations of life in a foreign land, Daniel remained faithful to God, as evidenced by his habit of praying three times per day. "Have you prayed your three times?" she'd ask.

Back then, I dismissed her reminders as the idle words of an aging loved one. But now I can see that Wavon was sharing wisdom passed to her, the best guidance she had to offer. Our family, like Daniel and his companions, lived in a land surrounded by danger on all sides. Given what was coming, my best chance of survival was prayer to the God who rescued an exile from the mouths of lions.

CHAPTER 2

Single Moms Aren't Allowed to Die

S unday service in the Anglican tradition calls for confession. Together as a congregation, we confess "the things done, and the things left undone," believing that the good we fail to do can mar our lives as much as the harm we inflict on ourselves and others.

My dad caused havoc in our family. That part of the story is easy enough to tell. But his absence during my childhood and teenage years created as many problems as his presence. It wasn't so much *him* that I missed. The loss of what my father could have done right was as impactful as the things he did wrong.

The first ramification showed up in the lack of money. With my father in and out of the house, the burden of financial support fell to my mother. When I was six years old, she found a job on a Chrysler assembly line, installing radios in automobiles. Once she'd won the trust of her bosses, they promoted her to the military division, where she soldered together metals to be used in cables for some unknown combat purpose. The money in the military division was better, and the extra income allowed her to save up enough for a down payment on a home.

The new neighborhood, the center of which was Sandia Boulevard, was a step up from where we had been. In our old neighborhood, patches of grass fought a losing battle with the dirt and the mud. But here, some homes had two stories, fresh coats of paint, and yards laid with green grass. Sandia and the surrounding streets were a "here comes everybody" neighborhood. Families with two-parent incomes had enough money to buy their kids name-brand clothes. Others, like us, saw Sandia as a sign that we were no longer completely broke. Still, the house was a stretch financially, and I remember my mother constantly being at work, taking extra shifts to pay for her children's sports and activity fees.

My siblings and I went to school every day, even if we were on death's doorstep, because there was no one at home to take care of us. School also meant food. Even when she worked full-time, my mother's income as a single parent qualified us for free breakfasts, courtesy of the U.S. government. At home, I ate off-brand cornflakes that turned to mush in my bowl no matter how quickly I gulped them down. At school, I normally chose the sausage-and-egg biscuits and drank a barely defrosted orange drink that resembled a slushy more than juice.

Revved up each morning on an infusion of quick sugar, I made my way to my classroom and stood for the Pledge of

Allegiance, led by our principal, who sounded barely intelligible over the PA system. Right hand over heart, I joined the groggy multitude for recitation. I had no idea what "justice for all" meant, but it must have been important, since we spoke about it every day.

Yet the first grade was also when I learned that my country had a malleable allegiance toward me and those who shared my complexion. Midway through one morning, after snack time but before lunch, my stomach began to ache. I suspect that the teachers at my school felt compelled to keep moderately sick kids in class, since illness meant a mother would miss work or the child would be left alone with nothing but a television as a babysitter—the calculus of caring for the offspring of the working poor. But noticing that my normally extroverted personality had become reserved, my teacher asked if I was okay. When I complained that my stomach hurt, she sent me to the office to call my mother.

I worried as I walked down the hall. My mom had told me never to call her at her job unless it was a true emergency, and I doubted a tummy ache would count. When I arrived at the office, the school secretary slid her rolling chair over to a file cabinet, pulled out my emergency contact form, and then dialed the Chrysler plant. She handed me the phone and it began to ring.

"Can I speak to Laurie McCaulley, please?" I asked when someone picked up the phone. I had already learned the manners that were necessary when speaking with a stranger. *Always use "sir" or "ma'am." End every request with "please." Do not use slang. Speak slowly, and do not jumble your words.* But this time the advice didn't help. "You have the wrong number," the man said, and he hung up the phone.

As I child, I showed fear by going completely still. I held the phone to my ear, trying to make sense of why the man had sounded so angry. Had my call interrupted a matter of great import?

I asked the office lady to call again, hoping that she had misdialed and not wanting to find myself on the phone with the angry man. Distressed, I took a deep breath and waited a second time for him to answer.

This time, his "Hello" had an edge to it. I tried again, hoping to win some sympathy. "I'm trying to reach my mom, Laurie McCaulley. She works at Chrysler. I'm her son Daniel and I'm sick."

"Don't you niggers know how to use the phone?" he spat. Then he slammed the receiver down again. The stillness returned, but now goosebumps appeared on my skin, and I shook with a surge of adrenaline. Seeing the look of terror on my face, the office lady asked me, "Baby, is everything okay?"

I mumbled yes, everything was fine. "Must be the wrong number." Then I exited the office as quickly as I could, the man's intimidating presence looming large in the room even after the call had ended.

The word *nigger* raised so many questions. I had always known I was Black, and I had heard older kids use the N-word before, but there was always a hint of playfulness when they said it. This time, the word was meant to shame and harm. To him, my Blackness was a bad thing. Why? His disgust was so convincing that I was tempted to believe that Blackness contained some irredeemable flaw.

Racism is not like puberty. You do not grow into it bit by bit, the way your body makes its way from the children's clothing section to the adults'. Anti-Blackness is more like the Big Bang, an explosion in which newly formed planets radiate out at light speed. Black children grow up fast because our flesh stirs up complex emotions in those much older than us. During the same years when we're memorizing vocabulary words and multiplication tables, we are also readying ourselves to read and respond to grown-up feelings.

That call would divide my Blackness in two. There was the Blackness of my community, of my grandfather's gospel quartet music, which he played whenever we visited his house, or the soul records my uncles forced me to listen to while insisting, "You don't know nothing 'bout this type of carrying on." This was the Blackness of tasting Aunt Mary's deep-fried catfish or Aunt Vanessa's red velvet cake after church, or listening to Marvin Gaye or Sam Cooke while waiting for the latest batch of meat off the grill. Then came the other Black: the way the outside world saw us. Black as danger or trouble. Black as an odd intrusion in a world that would be better off without us.

Before that call, I only knew Black as normal. But elementary school would introduce me to people outside my community. The rest of my life would be spent trying to be Black as I experienced Blackness, and not Black as white people—whatever their political persuasion—imagined Blackness to be.

Some years later, I still wonder what happened to the man on the phone. Did he live and die as angry as he appeared in that moment? Would he remember this incident for the rest of his life, or was that dispensation of racism as ordinary as a buy one, get one free sale at the Dollar Tree? I suspect he moved on and never revisited that moment.

On television, a boy who experienced something that frightened him would come home and tell his dad. But I had no father to talk to about my newfound Blackness. I could not ask my father to tell me when he'd discovered that the world saw him that way. Nor did I confide in my mom. Children of single parents learn to dole out their traumas in small doses. When I saw her that evening and she asked how my day had been, I said, "It was fine." I knew she carried a heavy load, and I wanted her to believe that her sacrifice was working.

My father, then, hadn't just closed himself off from us; he had in part closed me off from my mother. My mom never knew that her seven-year-old son found out that he was Black as the world defines it while he was sick and calling for her help. That lie of omission was the first of many lies created out of love for her. All of this meant that I, like other children of single parents, became independent before I was ready and able.

My mom worked to pay the bills, buy us reasonable clothes, and keep the refrigerator stocked. It was a delicate situation, one that held together until my mother got switched to the night shift. After that, her workday started before we got home from school and ended after we were asleep. She worked from three P.M. to eleven P.M., and sometimes past midnight, leaving my older sister, Latasha, in charge during the evenings.

Periodically, my mother would wake us up with a surprise when she arrived home late at night. I can still hear her voice saying, "I brought you all a treat" as she dragged us from the land of dreams to breakfast sandwiches and doughnuts of every variety: chocolate-covered, cream-filled, and glazed.

After we'd wolfed down those doughnuts, going back to sleep felt impossible. So we'd watch a movie or chat a bit before going back to bed. I thought it odd that she'd give us sweets late at night, when normally such pleasures were forbidden. It wasn't until later that I understood that those late-night meals were her chance to spend time with us.

But parenting via late-night doughnuts had its limitations. Without my mother at home to enforce the rules, I stopped doing my homework. My older sister was technically in charge, but I didn't want to listen to her. I didn't want a surrogate parent; I needed a real one. Latasha's command "Clean your room" was met with "You are not my mom!" "Have you done your homework?" gave way to "That's none of your business."

At the time, my father wasn't exactly gone; he was just insubstantial. He would come home for a few months, then turn abusive and leave. Regular drug use made him shrink. He lost the vigor and fearfulness of a new addict and took on the haggard appearance of a longtime one. Instead of being afraid of violence, I learned to watch for theft. If we weren't careful, our video game systems and VCRs disappeared.

Sometimes he was gone for months, other times for

more than a year. I missed him when he was away. During his absences, I could imagine a life with the father I knew as kind. When he came home, I remembered why I loathed him. This instability took its toll on me. My grades faltered, and teachers reported that I was acting out in class.

Picture day in fourth grade marked a turning point. According to my mother, I had to be dressed in my best outfit because that photo would become part of the yearbook, a keepsake that parents and students would remember forever. She declared, "I ain't having my son in that yearbook looking any kinda way."

Against my repeated protests, she forced me to put on my shiny black dress shoes and a pair of blue pants normally reserved for church, along with a white button-down shirt, a clip-on tie, and a vest. The full extent of her miscalculation became clear when I arrived at school. Most of the other kids' parents either hadn't known about picture day or hadn't cared, because my classmates all showed up in jeans, T-shirts, or tracksuits.

It did not take long for kids to note my resemblance to a preacher or a funeral home director. I quickly became "Pass-ah Esau," someone to be greeted with an exaggerated southern drawl and mocking laughs. I could have ignored that, having been called much worse before. But then a kid stalked up from behind and pushed me—and because the soles of my shoes were slippery, I fell over. Everyone started laughing, and I lost it. I jumped to my feet and rushed the kid, swinging wildly. He had the presence of mind to pull my vest over my head so that I couldn't see, but that didn't matter. I tackled him to the ground and kept punching.

By the time the teacher separated us, I had a bloody lip, but the other kid had one, too, and more scratches than I did. Apparently, I had won the fight.

I was dragged to the principal's office, where an administrator woke my mom from her post-late-shift sleep and told her to come get her son because he had been suspended. Although the drive from our house to the school couldn't have been longer than ten minutes, the time I spent waiting for her arrival felt eternal. I feared my mother's anger, but when she walked into the principal's office, I saw something worse: fatigue. Even though her posture was straight and alert, her eyes betrayed a lack of sleep and her voice had none of its usual energy.

She listened dutifully as the principal explained what had happened. I remember her apologizing for taking so much of his time, clearly wanting to get out of the building as quickly as possible. My mother has always been big on decorum, and I wondered if she was saving her fury for after we were out of earshot of the administrators. But she had little if anything to say to me on the car ride home. When we arrived, she sent me to my room and went back to sleep.

She later told me, "I couldn't get too mad at you because I blamed myself. I knew you were angry about your father. You may not remember this, but we actually put you in therapy for anger management around this time. It didn't last. You said you didn't like the counselor. I decided that I needed to change jobs or risk losing touch with all of you."

Changes at Chrysler gave my mother a chance to shift careers. With the rise in automation and the loss of crucial contracts, the company found itself overstaffed and began offering employees buyouts that carried one year's salary. My mom, who was making $28,000 per year, decided to take the buyout and use that money to go back to college. This seemed like a good plan: she'd get a job that allowed her to work while we were in school and spend time with us in the evenings. But such a plan was not to be. Shortly after the buyout, she began to feel ill. She had trouble getting out of bed in the morning and wore down easily. Normally, she kept track of how much television we watched and how many video games we played during the week. Now she began sleeping in the afternoon instead of supervising us. Her movements slowed. She would begin washing the dishes after dinner, then stop and sit down, as if she found the activity too tiring.

She attributed her fatigue to the fact that she was transitioning to a regular sleeping schedule after so many late nights. But then her legs started to swell, and her friends noticed a change in her complexion. One day I overheard Grandma Laura asking, "How can you be Black and pale? You need to go and see somebody." Mom complained to her doctor of headaches and told him that she felt like water was dripping behind her eyes. But he did not take her seriously and sent her home with advice to rest or take some Advil.

Eventually, after numerous tests, including three CT scans and an EKG, none of which revealed any problems, she started having seizures and momentary blindness. Still the doctors dismissed her concerns. One even suggested that she might be suffering from hysterical blindness and referred her to a psychiatrist. My mother pleaded, "I am not crazy, I'm dying!"

Everything came to a head one afternoon in late November, when she went Christmas shopping with my older sister, Latasha, and my aunt Linda Kay. They went into the Sears Surplus outlet, the discount store where Sears sent items with minor defects, looking for a talking baby doll—the hot toy that Christmas—for my sister Marketha. The doll was easy enough to find, but as Mom continued on, searching for some husky-sized pants for me, her vision went blurry. She told my aunt, "I am going to need you to buy these items for me with my credit card because I can't see." Linda Kay thought she was kidding until my mother rammed into a display. Troubled, Linda Kay and Latasha made the purchases and rushed her out of the store and to the hospital.

Now that she was blind, the doctors finally took my mother's case seriously. She would be in the hospital for a few days, so my siblings and I went to stay at my grandparents'. None of the adults told us what was going on. My grandparents only said, "Your mom is in the hospital for tests." I'm guessing they thought they were being kind by hiding the hard details from us, but the lack of information encouraged my imagination to run wild. Was she dying? My mom had always been a rock; she never got sick or missed work. Now our only remaining parent was in the hospital, and we didn't know why. I made promises to God: *If you just make sure that my mother is okay, I will be the perfect kid. I'll happily endure church every Sunday. I'll do all my homework and never be mean to my sisters.* I made meager offerings in exchange for my mother's life, because that was all that I had.

An extensive workup revealed that she had a tumor pressing on the nerves connecting her brain to her eyes. The "water" dripping behind her eyes had been blood. Her tumor had been hemorrhaging for weeks. The doctors scheduled surgery for January and informed her that she would remain without sight until then. Returning to Sandia was impossible. We would have to stay with Grandma Laura and Grand-dad Theodore until after the surgery.

Our move into my grandparents' house more than doubled the occupants. Where there had been three people living in a four-bedroom home (my grandparents and Aunt Mary, my grandmother's sister), now there were eight of us. My mom, having grown up there, knew every square inch of the house. That made getting around easier for her, despite her lack of vision. Nonetheless, she needed our help. As the older children, Latasha and I took turns helping her find her way to the couch or into a dining room chair without falling. For the first time in our lives, we did not need reminding to clean up after ourselves; we tidied the living room constantly, making sure shoes and toys were not left behind, where they might be in her path. I took on the task of pouring my mom cereal each morning, something she had done for me a thousand times, and then watched with concern as she dipped the spoon in and out of the milk, rarely managing to get a mouthful of cereal before she gave up.

The doctor had told my mother that the chances of her recovering her sight were not good and that she might die on the operating table, but the day before the procedure my mom made no grand declarations of love in case things went poorly. She merely said, "I have to go and have a surgery, and then I'll come back. Do not worry, God will take care of us."

I believed her.

Years later, when I was in college, she would tell me the full story of that day, confiding, "I was much more afraid than I let on, but I couldn't afford to show it to you all." My mom lied to protect our feelings, much like I had lied to protect hers years before. She remembered having a conversation with God before the nurses took her in: "I was laying on that cold, uncomfortable bed in that hospital gown, waiting for them to come get me. I had wires and stuff coming in and out of me. I was shaking a little with fear. I did what I always do when I am scared. I talked to God. *Lord, you know that I'm a crazy Black woman. You said that these children are a blessing. I didn't say that. You said it. And so if you want to leave me here to take care of them, I am okay with that.*"

She told me, "I heard from the Lord. I know it was the Lord because he pronounced my name correctly. He called me Laurie Ann. He said, *Lo, I will be with you forever and when I heal you, you will serve my children.*"

That encounter calmed her spirit, and when the nurses arrived to cart her off to brain surgery, she was ready.

The surgery was successful. A few hours later, when the anesthesia began to wear off, she slowly made her way back to consciousness, and for the first time in months, hazy figures resolved into human shapes. "I would have shouted if I could move," she says, "but I was too tired. So, I just praised God on the inside. He saw my heart dance, even if no one else could."

Ever the evangelist, my mom turned her homecoming three days later into a testimony. She said, "The Good Lord guided the hands of the surgeon, and I am all right now. We are going to be okay."

But subsequent tests would show that her healing had not been complete. She had lost her peripheral vision; she could no longer see us out of the corners of her eyes. There were other, hidden changes as well. The tumor had damaged her pituitary gland, leaving it nonfunctional. She would need a cocktail of drugs to keep her blood pressure from spiking. If she got overheated, her sweat glands could go haywire, causing her to lose most of the fluid in her body. Since stressful situations threw her body out of whack, making the medications less effective, her doctor advised her not to work. My mother had lived, but things would not be going back to normal.

What came next was less food and more insecurity. Instead of the Chrysler pay or the money from the new career she'd envisioned after college, we would live on her disability check of $1,600 per month, which came to $19,200 a year—a hard drop from the $28,000 we'd been scraping by on. Meanwhile, my father lived in a series of low-budget hotels, the power of his addiction waxing and waning with the seasons. He would come home for a few days, and my mother would welcome him in. But he never stayed for long. Once while my mother slept, he found the drugs the doctor had prescribed her and took them. She woke up to the sight of him in the corner of her bedroom shivering and complaining, "It feels like my brain is shaking."

She threw him out again, and we struggled on by ourselves.

My family went on government assistance in the era of the "welfare queen," when radio and television hosts garnered ratings by stirring up contempt for people like my mother. Politicians declared that compassion toward families such as mine encouraged laziness, and this argument carried them into statehouses and governors' mansions. In the prevailing view, poverty was not the problem to be addressed; the American people needed to be protected from Black single mothers and their children. Instead of working to provide better lives for their families, these women robbed the federal government and benefited from the efforts of others. For them, with four kids, no husband, and no college degree, my mom was the myth made flesh.

This trope didn't just attach to her; it spread out to us. As children of a single mother, we were doomed as well. According to the statistics, my brother and I were destined for jail and my sisters for teenage pregnancy. It felt as if practically the whole of society was waiting for us to fail, so that people could say, "We told you so, and this is why we shouldn't help." Thinking about this made me angry, but I also thought of my father. My mother could do nothing about her tumor, but my father was a different story. He played a starring role in our clichéd drama by means of his absence. Living as a stereotype taught me a valuable lesson: if people were wrong about my mother and her challenges, then they were also probably wrong about me and a host of other Black people they categorized and dismissed.

For my family, no formal announcement told us that we were now even poorer. I knew it because we ate out much less frequently, and the purchase of M&M's and Kit Kats during gas station fill-ups came to an end. One Saturday we went to a church down the road from where we lived. It was not our normal place of worship, nor was it Sunday, so I wondered why we were there. Inside the church, a makeshift grocery store with eggs, butter, sugar, and peanut butter had been set up on folding tables. But there was no place to pay. Instead of a cash register, I saw a bunch of shamefaced kids avoiding eye contact, having realized before I did that this was a charity event. I looked up at my mom; her mood always set the tone for my own. If she was sad or scared, her face betrayed no emotion. Despite her strength, I wanted to disappear. A sense of worry and profound sadness pressed down on my shoulders, but she went about the work of filling the basket with the items we would need. My mother couldn't afford to be too proud; she had hungry children to feed.

Three Inches to the Right

During the planning of my father's eulogy, I found out that he had never graduated from high school. Neither had his father or his grandfather. Looking back, this fact made sense of certain childhood memories. My father did not read to me or engage me in conversations about the life of the mind. He never spoke to me about college or my dreams for the future. If he nursed aspirations of his own, he never shared them with his son. As far as I could tell, he took each day as it came. He was either on the road or at home with a beer in his hand, watching TV.

Still, when I started my freshman year of high school, I did not know that I was entering a place from which the men on my father's side of the family had never exited.

I began my secondary education at Johnson High, the

same school my mother graduated from the year I was born. The two-story building's most notable feature was its mascot, the Jaguar, painted in bright blue and gold on the basketball court's hardwood floor. Pride for the blue and gold was, in effect, Black pride among the thirteen hundred students crammed into its classrooms and hallways. The Jaguars had a long history of excelling in sports—especially basketball and football. Most every academically eligible Black male of any athletic ability in my neighborhood went out for a team, in part because sports were a pathway to local status and, potentially, a college scholarship.

There was a robust Black intellectual life, too; we might argue about Langston Hughes and Paul Laurence Dunbar in the classroom and discuss the racial politics of Spike Lee's *Do the Right Thing* at lunch. If you cared about school, that was fine enough. But those books, formulas, equations, and history lessons had to answer the most pressing questions: *What are we doing here in this school? What is the point?* If you were religious, your classmates wanted to know: *What does your God know or have to say about crack babies or police stops for driving while Black?* Questions of life and death, hope and despair were tossed around like footballs in the backyard on a Saturday afternoon. I have never experienced that much multifaceted intelligence, swagger, and potential in one place since. I found myself constantly pressed, emotionally and intellectually, to give an account of who I was, what I wanted to be, and how I might get there.

To the larger world, however, Johnson was known for its violence and its academic struggles. Consistently listed as one of the lowest-performing schools in a state whose rank-ing ranged from 47 to 49 out of the 50 in terms of quality of education, Johnson was often compared to Grissom, the majority-white school in the wealthy part of town and one of the top academic schools in the state. According to the media, we were the shame of the city and Grissom its glory.

TROUBLED JOHNSON HIGH SCHOOL ERUPTS IN VIOLENCE.

WHAT SHOULD BE DONE ABOUT FAILING SCHOOLS LIKE JOHN-SON? CLOSURE OR NEW LEADERSHIP?

GRISSOM LEADS THE WAY IN THE STATE OF ALABAMA.

GRISSOM HIGH HAS RECORD NUMBER OF NATIONAL MERIT SCHOLARS.

On my first day of ninth grade, my older sister, Latasha, pointed me toward the freshman hallway with a casual wave of the hand before trotting off to hang out with her crew. I searched frantically for a friendly face from middle school and spotted a few folks from the neighborhood. That calmed my anxiety enough that I could walk to my homeroom and try to settle down. Attendance was taken, followed by an an-nouncement that freshmen were to report to the audito-rium for a welcome from the principal.

A lot was said that morning, all of which I forgot except for one bit: *There are around four hundred of you in the audito-rium this morning. Four years from now, half of you will be gone. You will be either on the streets or in jail. I say this every year to try to convince some of you to take this seriously and try to make a life for yourself, but I know you won't listen. Prove me wrong.* Fresh out of middle school, more interested in the upcoming pep rally than existential questions about our future, most stu-dents laughed off the principal's speech. But I was surprised by his words. Half of us gone? I looked around and wondered, *Where could two hundred people disappear to?*

Though it seemed impossible, I believed him because he was the academic leader of the school. Why would he lie to us? From his speech, I understood that persistence was a matter of choice. Half of us would quit because we didn't want it bad enough. I was not yet mature enough to realize that things were not so simple.

Owing less to the principal's warning than to my mother's positive influence, I dreamed of college, even though I had little idea of how to get there. Some of my friends spoke about joining the military after high school; at two least guys I knew from my neighborhood would. Others planned on picking up trades or finding work where they could get it. That was fine; college is not for everyone. For others, school became a chance to have fun by inflicting emotional or physical harm on other Black teens. That was the part of Johnson I hated.

Over the next four years, I would witness fights that broke out between boys due to perceived acts of disrespect or jokes gone wrong. I would see girls circle each other with razor blades, striking and dodging, always aiming at the face. I can't count how many house parties or clubs I fled because someone pulled a gun or threatened to go to his car and obtain one. During lunch, a boy would be beaten bloody for no discernible reason. At football games, the parking lot or the concessions line would become a place to settle scores.

I feared the violence, but even more, I loathed it for the way it seemed to confirm the already negative opinion of Black students in Huntsville. Unfortunately, Black children are rarely ever individuals. If two kids at Johnson got into a fight, it reflected on more than just them; it spoke about our race and our worth as people. Blackness was forever on trial. I wondered why our successes didn't seem to work that way. A Black kid scoring high on the SAT was about an individual's ability to overcome Johnson High School, not the potential of a whole people.

I remember those fights not as a reason for Black shame but as manifestations of the cruelty that can cluster in spaces when hope has been taken away. To avoid processing our traumas, we made jokes about the violence, knowing in our hearts that there was nothing particularly funny about it. The common refrain was "You gotta stay ready in these streets—don't get caught slipping."

As a parent, my mom wanted more for the kids of Northwest Huntsville than violence and poverty. After her brain surgery, when the medications made it impossible for her to keep a steady job, she turned her focus to her children. "So many parents were struggling to figure out what to do," she said. "I started to volunteer at the school. I helped students with homework and just began to walk around and talk with people."

Her influence grew from there. She joined the PTA, became its president, and eventually was elected to the school board. Of that experience she said, "Once I joined the school board, it was like finding out about all the secrets that only white folks knew." Soon, my sister and I were enrolled in Advanced Placement classes for college credit. I would go to Boys State, a summer program where kids from all over Alabama went to learn about politics and civic engagement. My mother didn't explain it at the time, but she'd set about building my résumé piece by piece. I did what she told me to do because if I didn't, she wouldn't let me play football.

My mother turned education into the great test of who we were. She would come home from meetings with local politicians and say, "Some of them folks is so racist. I just had to pray for them. They said, 'Those kids in Northwest Huntsville couldn't learn or were too violent.' Is that true? Are you too violent? Are they smarter than you? Because I met some of them across town, and they as dumb as the day is long. If they are smarter than you, then I have failed you as a mother." I did not enter classes; I entered the arena. Black achievement battled against white racism on every test and paper. She dared us to prove everyone wrong. And that message wasn't just for her children. She used her perch as a PTA leader and school board member to preach the good news of Black intellectual possibility to any who would listen.

Neighborhood life became complicated around this time. Like a bunch of other mothers in my community, my mom had given birth to her first children as a teenager, which meant that by the time my friends and I reached high school, there were lots of single, attractive Black moms in their mid-thirties. Men in their mid-twenties would appear at our parties or at hangouts that should have been reserved for teens, and it disturbed us to watch their eyes lingering both on our mothers and on the teen girls we wanted to date.

A good friend of mine had one of those attractive moms. When she came to pick him up from school one day, a classmate saw her approach and asked, "Is that your momma?"

"Yes," he replied in a clipped tone that signaled his desire to end the conversation.

The classmate continued: "Can she come by my house and tutor me? There were a couple of things I learned in *health* class I would like her opinion on."

My friend stood ready to fight until his mother inserted herself. "Leave them *boys* alone," she said. "They ain't got nothing I want."

The classmate stormed off, threatening that he would *see* my friend at school the next day. He wasn't bluffing.

We Black teenage boys became more and more aware of our mothers' sacrifices as we aged. That was why we were so quick to fight anyone who disrespected our mothers. It's why rappers from the 1990s and 2000s wrote an endless stream of songs dedicated to mothers and the difference that maternal support makes in a young man's life and career. We had Tupac's "Dear Mama," Kanye's "Hey Mama," Goodie Mob's "Guess Who," and Snoop Dogg's "I Love My Momma." We knew through direct experience the pain women experienced when they had to raise children on their own. We *were* those children. But our love for our mothers did not cause us to reflect on how some of our attitudes about women in our community created the need for sacrificial single parenting.

My mom did not begrudge other women for trying to find love in new relationships, but she opted out of the whole enterprise. There would be no series of stand-in fathers to play the role of dad for a season, no strange men appearing at our breakfast table only to leave after a few months. The work of inspiring us to thrive academically seemed to be her only interest. After my father left, my mother never dated seriously again.

I never thought this odd when I was a preteen. The Bible tells the story of a woman named Hannah who longed for a child but couldn't get pregnant. Her husband, Elkanah, tried to comfort her, saying, "Hannah, why do you weep? . . . Am I not more to you than ten sons?" Like Elkanah, I did not recognize that my love could not solve the problem of my mother's loneliness. I promised her, "When I get rich, I am going to buy you a house, fancy clothes, anything you want." She'd smile at my declarations and say, "I'm sure you will, son."

Money can buy lots of things, but it cannot purchase time. It cannot give my mother back her youth. It cannot return the many years she spent without someone to tell her that her hair looked pretty on a Sunday afternoon. She gave up dinner dates, surprise gifts, and Valentine's cards—except those sketched on construction paper in the shaky script of a middle school boy. She made that sacrifice so that I could have a stabler life. She succeeded, but at what cost?

My mom would not want pity. She has too much pride for that. She always told us, "Whatever I had to go through with your dad, it gave me you four. Half the time y'all drive me crazy, but it's worth it." Her children were evidence that God could bring something beautiful out of the ruins of those years. But if we were the good thing that had come out of a season of suffering, then we had to be protected.

Maybe my mom's experience as a single mother led to her determined parenting of my sisters. She treated her daughters differently than her sons. As my older sister, Latasha, neared the end of high school—the same age my mother was when she got pregnant with her—my mother devoted her time to monitoring Latasha's relationships with young men.

Latasha had a natural grace, beauty, and confidence. Unlike me, she could clap on beat and knew all the freshest dances. Everyone loved her. She was a cheerleader and a straight-A student with enough sass that no one dared challenge her—except our mother. While some would rejoice at having gifted and beautiful daughters, my mother saw it as a danger, something that needed to be cordoned off from the world. She knew that their attractiveness made them a target.

I never had a curfew, but my sisters did. When I received a phone call, my mother didn't ask afterward who I'd been speaking with. But when my sister got a call, my mom would ask, "Who was that?" If it was a boy, she would follow up with "How old is he?" and "What does he want with my daughter?"

As the oldest of the male children, I was drafted into my mom's struggle with the constant admonition to "take care of your sister no matter what." Oddly enough, the same culture that taught me to prey on other people's daughters encouraged me to protect the women closest to me. In our music and movies, we too often depicted the journey from boyhood as one of sexual conquest. At school, guys teased each other: *What happened after you all left the party? Did she let you hit it?* But within our family, I was the man of the house. Even though she was two years older, Latasha became my responsibility.

The summer before my freshman year, she took me with her to see her boyfriend, Chris, who lived in the public housing projects across town. I had visited friends in these projects many times. The houses were built with the melancholic yellow bricks that could be found in housing projects all over America. The handful of nice yards dotting the area were usually cared for by elderly couples, left over from the time when the projects provided an opportunity for home ownership. Their interiors were snapshots of Black aspiration in the late 1960s, the walls adorned with pictures of Martin Luther King, Jr., blue-eyed and blond-haired Jesuses, and grandchildren who had graduated from high school or joined the military. Rotary phones still sat on end tables, large record players took up space in the living room, and the furniture was covered in plastic to keep the whole place pristine, if a little sterile. The homes of those grandparents were pockets of defiant hope. But that day we weren't visiting them. We stood, instead, on the corner outside, where teenagers gathered in clusters, tossing dice against the wall for cash and casually flirting with members of the opposite sex.

Latasha was excited to see Chris that day, but he showed up mad, complaining that he'd heard she was spending a lot of time with another boy.

An argument ensued. "I've known him my whole life," Latasha said. "We're just friends."

"I saw how he looked at you the other day. He has a crush on you."

"He does not, and I'm a grown woman. You can't tell me who I can and cannot talk to."

"B*tch, you better motherf*ckin' do what I say."

Before the argument, I'd been caught up in the dice game, absorbed by the sound of the dice bouncing on the concrete and the intrigue of seeing who would take home the wads of tens and twenties. One of the players had mastered the technique, rolling seven after seven.

As Latasha's and Chris's voices picked up, my attention turned to them. My sister was unbothered by his words, giving as good as she got. But when he cursed at my sister and put his finger in her face, I ran at him with all the rage and intimidation I could muster. A few inches taller than me, Chris outweighed me by a significant amount, and that difference became more apparent as I approached with violent intent. But there was no turning back now, so I yelled, "You can't talk to my sister like that!" My fists were balled, ready to defend my sister's honor.

Latasha's eyes widened. She reached for Chris to try to talk to him, but surrounded by his neighborhood friends, he was past that now. He must have known that I had no ability to carry out my threat. Many years younger and much smaller, I posed no real danger to him. But respect was the currency of exchange in the cultural economy of the projects, and I had publicly disrespected him. He could never allow that to stand. He hit me across the face, and I fell to the ground. The crowd erupted—*Ooooh!*—in the rush of excitement that accompanies the beginning of a fight.

Pain radiated from my cheek down through my legs, depriving them of strength through the strange alchemy that occurs when agony mixes with fear. My body trembled. I began to weep, not simply from the sting, but from the sheer ridiculousness of it all. What was I doing here?

That afternoon, I was not just one teenager trying to fight a much older drug dealer. I was all the helpless little boys who couldn't protect the women they loved. I couldn't protect my mother when my father came home high and violent. I couldn't protect my sister from a man who didn't treat her well.

Chris stood over me, his face more playful than deadly. My life was not in danger, but it seemed clear that he would kick me a few times and leave me with bruised ribs and a swollen cheek, possibly a black eye.

Then a voice from the ether said, "Hey, leave that young fella alone. He was just defending his sister. Why you trying to fight a child?"

I crawled away while Chris and the other guy traded insults and threats. Having no idea where to go, I wandered through the projects with a sore cheek and wounded pride until Latasha's car came creeping toward me. "Daniel, get in the car," she said through the open window. "We need to go home."

Having spent my bravado attempting to play the man of the house and defend her honor, I responded like a petulant child: "I'm not going home. Leave me here. I'll be fine."

My sister took a softer tone: "Thank you for standing up for me. I'm proud of you, but you could have been hurt. Next time let me take care of it."

"I'm never going to let anyone disrespect my sister!" I protested.

"I know, Daniel." Frustrated as she might have been, Latasha managed to keep her voice neutral and her tone calm and reasonable. "Get in the car. Mom is expecting us home soon."

I slumped into the passenger seat and stared out the window, refusing to make eye contact while at the same time feeling thankful that she didn't say anything else, the radio and the air conditioner filling the silence as we made our way home.

I'm guessing many Black women have had to do what Latasha did for me that afternoon: help the men in their lives feel okay for not being able to protect them. I used to pray that I would grow big and strong enough to win a fight like that. I realize now that the problem wasn't merely the limitation posed by my size. The problem was the limited tools and imagination that made violence the only solution. The problem was the widespread lack of respect for Black women that allowed my sister's boyfriend to call her something so vile. The problem was my inability to see that, at bottom, he and I weren't combatants. We were fellow prisoners to a toxic definition of manhood, struggling for the remnants of respect left after a society had stripped us of dignity. We should have questioned the system.

Rather than breaking up, my sister and Chris started hanging out together again within a matter of days, and Chris and I settled into an uneasy truce. Whenever he visited, he and my sister would take over the living room couch and I would retreat to my room to watch TV. It went on this way until one evening a few months later, after the start of school. With my mother gone to the Winn-Dixie to buy groceries, Latasha and Chris, Marketha, Brandon, and I were alone in the house. I was sitting on my twin bed watching television when the noise of a gunshot erupted from somewhere outside the house. The next thing I knew, bullets were piercing the wall to my room.

As I watched holes appear, I had a feeling of utter calm. I thought, *They are shooting up the entire house, so it makes no sense to duck or hit the ground.*

Once the noise subsided, I came back to myself. Realizing others in the house might be hurt, I rushed to the living room. Relieved to see that Latasha was fine, I then ran to the back of the house and found that Marketha and Brandon were unharmed as well.

My mother returned to cop cars up and down the block, horrified that our home had become a crime scene. With groceries in her arms, she interrupted the police officers who had gathered us in the front room, trying to comfort us. "What happened here?" she asked, breathing hard.

"Can I speak to you in private for a moment?" a Black officer said.

She nodded, put down her groceries, and withdrew with the officer to the kitchen for a conversation I overheard. "Ma'am, do you know who you have in your house?" the officer asked, looking into the room where we sat with Chris.

"Yes," she said. "That's just my daughter's latest boyfriend."

The officer explained, "That young man leads one of the major gangs in the city, and he is in conflict with another group. Your children are lucky to be alive."

My mother looked toward the living room, where Latasha was busy tending to a minor scrape on Chris's arm. When she saw the two of them, she lost it. "You all could have died!" she screamed, and she charged at my sister. The officers pulled her back, and she collapsed in tears.

Later that night, returning to my room still in shock, I studied the bullet holes in the wall of my bedroom. One in particular caught my attention. It was about three inches to the right of where my head had been. I do not know what caused me to remain still while shots were being fired, but I have always wondered: From where did the calm arise? Had I moved a few feet this way or that, my life would have ended that night.

I imagined how the newspapers would have reported my death: BLACK YOUTH KILLED IN DRIVE-BY SHOOTING. CRIME OUT OF CONTROL IN NORTHWEST HUNTSVILLE. Would a radio host, commenting on the story, suggest that I'd gotten what I'd deserved for associating with a known felon? In the early 1990s, when it was okay for the mainstream media to frame Black teenagers as predators, would anyone have pressed to learn the truth of my story?

The shooting happened not long after the principal addressed the freshman class. Little did I know then that four years later, he would end up being correct. At graduation, only about two hundred of our class of four hundred remained. Some of us were in jail, and a few of us had died.

But in another, crucial way, he was wrong: it wasn't necessarily a question of who took his speech seriously. We who lived did not do so because we made the right decisions. Sometimes we were just as foolish as those who faltered. I did not feel like I represented the best of us when I walked across the stage to receive my diploma. I felt responsible, and I wondered what those other two hundred might have become had we lived in a world that didn't demand so much of us when all we were trying to do was be kids.

CHAPTER 4

The Game Is Undefeated

From the age of five until my twenty-second year, I spent my autumns on football fields. As a chubby elementary and middle schooler, I started out as a lineman, charged with protecting quarterbacks from rushing defenders and clearing the way for the running backs. My role began to change during the transition from middle to high school, when coaches from Johnson High came to watch us practice as a way of scouting for next year's team. Eager to impress our future coaches, we sprinted harder and tackled with more vigor.

After the drills one day, the defensive coach came over to me and said, "I think you could be a good defender, possibly even a linebacker if you dedicate yourself."

Excited at the prospect of being something other than a glorified bodyguard, I said, "Tell me what I need to do."

"Get your body into shape over the summer. Lose fifteen to twenty pounds."

"Give me a workout to do, and I will, sir."

A few days later, he returned with a packet full of instructions on how many sprints to run and push-ups to do; it also included a full weight-lifting workout. There was a saying in my neighborhood: "You can either preach, play ball, or sell dope." Only the first two gave you a realistic chance of leaving the neighborhood.

The drug game ended undefeated. As they say in poker, "The house always wins." I didn't know an old drug dealer. I could not recall any who had gathered up a nest egg and retired peacefully to the suburbs, but I was well acquainted with those who'd gotten arrested and done a bid downstate. I'd also seen dealers slowly slip from selling to becoming addicts themselves. As a pure matter of statistics, selling drugs seemed like a path to madness.

But if you could play ball, you could go to college or the pros. We knew that the odds of making it to the NBA or NFL were slim, but in a context where anything ending well seemed unlikely, professional sports appeared to be as good a bet as any.

I studied the workout pamphlet the coach had given me, and by the end of the summer the transformation of my body had begun. I had lost enough weight and gained enough quickness to play linebacker on defense. That was a much better position, because I would max out at five foot eleven, meaning I had no chance of getting a scholarship as an offensive lineman. Division I guards are usually six foot three or above and weigh around three hundred pounds. My freshman year, I was five-eight, two hundred pounds. Although I knew that linebackers were usually over six feet tall, I took some comfort when I later reached five-eleven, making me taller than Sam Mills, the star linebacker for the New Orleans Saints.

Only a few hundred fans attended the freshmen football games, but as I made my way from junior varsity to varsity, the crowds grew. Most of our games took place in Milton Frank Stadium, a venue that held twelve thousand people, shared by many of the schools in Huntsville. When we played our rivals, we could be assured that the stands would be packed.

As the crowd size increased from a few dedicated parents to whole stadiums, my anger at my father grew. It seemed like the whole city was coming to see us play, but he couldn't make it. He had a thousand different reasons for missing my games. He was in jail or at work or strung out or mad at my mother or bored or simply uninterested. Still, I made it a part of my pregame habit to look for his face in the crowds, and I let my fury about his absence fuel my play, taking my frustrations out on the quarterbacks and running backs I chased around the field. When I made a sack or recovered a fumble, I'd hear in the roaring crowd the missing voice of the man who took me to my first practice.

My mother knew how much his absence hurt me, even if we never spoke about the matter. That might have been the reason her face appeared every time I looked into the stands, smiling and laughing with the other parents, decked out in blue and gold. Only later would she confide that she never much liked football. "Half the time I didn't know what was going on. This is what I did: I saw you run into a pile of bodies. If you got up, I cheered because that meant you were okay."

Other moms and dads weren't so indifferent. Coaches needed thick skin to deal with aggressive parents postgame:

Why didn't you run the ball more?

What kind of defensive scheme are we running out there?

Either my son starts getting playing time or we will move him to a school that recognizes his talent.

I remember the coach's response when the dad of a friend confronted him over why his son wasn't thrown the ball more often: "Well, first of all, he's as slow as molasses, so he's never open. When he is open and we throw it to him, he drops it half the time. So we don't throw it to your son because I'm interested in winning football games." Most of the team heard this exchange, and quite a few of us began to chuckle. The father didn't ask any more questions about his son after that.

This intensity around youth sports started early. My sophomore year, I worked as a Little League baseball referee to make extra money. I think I got paid $30 a game. Most of the action played out like a comedy of errors. If by some miracle a kid managed to make good contact with the baseball and it went beyond the dirt surrounding the bases, there was about a 25 percent chance that an outfielder would accurately throw the ball to the infield. It was even less probable that said infielder would catch the ball.

What should have been singles routinely turned into inside-the-park home runs, with boys rounding the bases as the ball flew wildly from panicked kid to panicked kid. But not always. During one game, a child hit a grounder to the second baseman. The second baseman caught it cleanly, much to my shock, then tossed a wobbly ball toward the first baseman, who also held on to it. Meanwhile, the youth who'd hit the baseball had been sprinting as fast as his legs could take him down the first-base line, resulting in the most unlikely of events: a bang-bang play in recreation league baseball. Having no idea if the runner was safe, I called the kid out, impressed to see such a clean throw and catch in Little League.

The children on the field that day ranged probably from seven to eight years old. The stakes could not have been lower. Nonetheless, a flurry of invective came flying from the stands.

He was clearly safe!

He beat that tag by a mile. Have you ever played baseball? Did you see it?

I tell you what, you better not miss another call like that.

Where do they find these refs?

I wanted to reply: *They found us in the same neighborhoods that produced the athletes. I'm just trying to help and make a little money. Calm down.*

The fury seemed odd then—more befitting of an NCAA championship than a Little League scrimmage—but now I understand. Fathers and mothers fought for their children to be given the chance to show what they could do, because each at bat, from Little League to high school, each touchdown or tackle, felt like a step toward financial security.

Still, despite the central role it played in our lives, sports could be a fickle monster. Our neighborhoods were filled with former athletes who could tell us about how they "almost made it." Some of the reasons given for why things didn't work out:

1. The coach didn't recognize my skills.
2. Man, it was all politics. He played me out of position.
3. I had a full-ride offer from Tennessee, then I got this girl pregnant. I had to drop out to take care of my kid.
4. I couldn't pass the SAT, so they pulled my scholarship.
5. Bro, I got arrested for something I didn't even do and they kicked me off the team.
6. I had all the talent in the world, but I never worked at it. I didn't take it seriously enough.

Despite their bad luck, these guys said things would be different for us. We wouldn't get hurt. The coach would help us build our skills, and we would go to college.

Every week when I was walking through the church lobby or traveling around the neighborhood, an adult would ask me, "How is football going? You keep it up, you'll get a Division I scholarship."

They also cautioned me about my academics: "Now, you need to keep those grades up so you will qualify. They don't wanna give no full rides to dummies. Ain't no use of you doing all this just to flunk out of school."

My mom understood that football was my focus, but she liked to say, "Your brain was made for more than smashing your head into piles of bodies." She made a habit of bragging to her friends in my presence when I did well on a test. She never talked to them about how I played on Friday nights.

My sophomore year, I became privy to how small changes could send an athlete tumbling when the city increased the minimum number of required courses for school sports. Where it used to be that you had to pass four of seven courses to be eligible to play (technically three, since you could make up a failed course during summer school), now it was five; the school board claimed it needed to ensure that those involved in sports took school seriously.

Still, there is a fine line between holding people account-able and crushing their souls. The old policy enabled athletes to struggle along, passing three classes during the year and a fourth during the summer—just enough to stay on the team—until they arrived at their senior year with nearly enough credits to graduate. Every year former athletes would visit us at practice and say, "Thank you, Coach, for using football to keep me in school until I figured out I could do more than run and tackle." Then they'd turn to us and say, "You all listen to your coaches, not just about sports but life." The game was more than just a way to build fitness or character. It was about fighting for a wider life.

Coaches, often more than clergy, served as our counsel-ors and therapists. We would go into their offices and tell them about our girl problems or issues at home that made practice difficult. They knew when we couldn't afford cleats or when there wasn't enough food to keep our growing bod-ies well fed. They carried us kicking and screaming through high school. Sports were a gateway drug to education. If the coach found out that we'd missed an assignment, he'd punish us by giving us extra laps. It was a well-known rule that if you skipped class on game day you might not get to play that evening. We feared our coaches' wrath more than our teachers'.

That's what those outside our community didn't understand. We weren't dumb or incapable. We just needed a reason to believe, and sports were that chance.

The change in course requirements meant that some of my teammates would simply quit. One day after the new policy was announced, I stopped a friend as he was turning in his equipment. "Man, hold up," I said. "Where you going? Don't quit. We got a great chance to win state next year. Let me holla at Coach, he'll figure something out. You know he got our backs."

The look in my friend's eyes made it evident that I was wasting my time. "Nah, man, I'm good. I can't pass no five classes," he said. He walked away and soon dropped out of school. We lost contact after that. A few years later, I heard that he'd been shot and killed in a robbery gone wrong.

Sports did more than inspire us to stay in school; they served as an actual refuge. Practice kept us off the streets and under supervision. For working-class parents, the gap from three-thirty to five-thirty P.M. —between the end of school and the end of their shifts—is fraught with danger. It's no coincidence that a significant proportion of juvenile crime happens during those afternoon hours.* What better time to

---

* For more information, see this report from Fight Crime: Invest in Kids: https://www.ojp.gov/ncjrs/virtual-library/abstracts/americas -after-school-choice-prime-time-juvenile-crime-or-youth.

break into a home than when you know the owners aren't present? What better time to settle scores than when you catch someone walking home alone after school? Practice did more than improve our skills; it extended our safety until the evening.

I was not an excellent student in high school, but I did well enough. Some football schools, like Vanderbilt, had stringent academic requirements. I hoped that the combination of on-field success and decent grades would win me a scholarship to one of those universities. I still didn't see my academic abilities as my sole hope, but in combination with football, college seemed attainable. I'd get a scholarship playing football, major in history, then earn my teaching certificate and find a job as a high school football coach. Football had been my way out; I'd use sports to help Black boys like me out of neighborhoods like the one I grew up in, just like my coaches did for me.

My junior year was looking good. Our team was ranked No. 2 in the state. The quarterback was a six-foot-five athlete with a rocket arm. He would go on to sign with Mississippi State and start all four years, leading them to three straight bowl games and one Southeastern Conference Championship appearance. Our leading receiver was six-one, 180 pounds of muscle, and could run like the wind. He likely would have signed with a major program, too, had his grades not gotten in the way. Instead, he became a standout at Alabama A&M, the HBCU in the city. Besides these two stars, our team featured players who would be awarded college scholarships all over the South: Louisville, Tennessee, Alabama A&M, University of Alabama at Birmingham, University of North Alabama.

Amid all that talent, I held my own, leading the team in tackles and functioning as a play caller on defense. At home, I kept a box under my bed with all the letters of interest I received from colleges. After school and practice I would retreat to my room, close the door, and lie on the twin bed, which now barely fit me, reading the letters over and over and daydreaming about life on a college campus as a star athlete. Alone with my bounty of papers, I figured it was okay to feel just a bit giddy.

What I cherished even more were the phone calls. College recruiting is a lot like dating. When the coaches phoned, they'd ask about sports, but they also wanted to know about my life and my goals. I'd play along, hoping to get invited on an official visit, since I knew that to be when most offers were made.

I believed it would happen for me. Most teams we played that year simply had no chance. We were too fast and athletic. Our QB would drop back and release a perfect spiral as the star receiver glided up the sideline. No matter how talented the opponent's corner, the receiver would simply jump over him and take the ball. On defense, we could not be blocked. We plowed through opposing linemen, sacking the quarterback and tossing running backs to the ground.

Our band, too, was in rare form that year. The musicians played instrumental renditions of the latest hip-hop and R&B songs, mixed in with hits from the seventies. Each game had the feel of a party. The crowd favorite was "So

Glad to See You Again." The beat was set to the *whomp*s of the tuba and the pounding bass of the drum, our dance team leading the way with hips and hair shaking to the chorus the band had modified for our school: "So glad to see you again / I haven't seen you since I don't know when / We are the J.O. Jaguar Band / We are the best band, best band in the land." It was as if God, knowing this to be a supreme sports moment in Northwest Huntsville, had given us a band to match our talent. Caught up in the music, I would dance between the plays.

But my dream of a college scholarship would fall to pieces the night we played Shades Valley. Right before half-time, I was on the sidelines waiting for the clock to wind down so I could head into the locker room when Coach sent me back in, saying, "Make sure they don't get nothing cheap before the half."

I could tell our opponents were going to throw, based on their formation. One of my gifts as a player was knowing what the other team was going to do because I watched so much film to prep. I said to the corner, "Watch the fade route." They snapped the ball and, sure enough, it was a pass. The quarterback rolled to the right, and I drifted along with him while I dropped back in coverage. He couldn't find anyone open, so he decided to run for it. I closed the distance, ready to make an open-field tackle. Right before he got to me, he decided to slide and avoid the hit. What I didn't see was that my friend and teammate Petty was chasing him from behind. Petty dived for the tackle and flew over the sliding quarterback, right into my knee.

The collision of his helmet into my leg felt like being

struck by lightning. Pain flared everywhere. My mother saw me go into the pile of bodies, and this time I didn't get up. Never in twelve years of playing football had I been seriously injured. I tried to stand, but my knee gave way. I slumped back onto the ground.

Two teammates arrived and helped me off the field, one on each side. I couldn't place any weight on my leg, but, surprisingly, the pain was gone. I am not sure whether it was shock or tremendous sadness that pushed away all other sensations. When I made it to the sidelines, I noticed that the cheerleaders had stopped their routines. Their shaking pom-poms had stilled, and all I saw was worry. Tracy, one of the girls I knew from history class, began to cry. Those tears let me know I was definitely in trouble.

They took me to the hospital to have my leg examined, and I listened to the rest of the game on the radio. We won a nail-biter, 17–14. The doctors took X-rays and told me that they would need a few days to determine the extent of the damage. I went home like a person convicted of a crime: I knew that I was guilty; the only question was the length of my sentence.

The following Monday my teammates and coaches tried to console me:

Don't worry, you'll bounce back.

Maybe you'll hear good news from the docs. Keep your head up.

I had a cousin that hurt his knee and came back stronger and faster.

Then came the verdict. I had torn three ligaments in my left knee: the ACL, MCL, and PCL. The doctor called it "the unholy trinity." I didn't know how many ligaments were in a knee, but that didn't sound good. I had one question for the doctor: "When can I get back on the field?"

"Unfortunately, we can't get you into surgery until January," he began. "It's usually nine months of rehab before you can begin football activities, twelve months before you can play in a game. That's with top-flight access to therapy. We are still trying to figure that out, due to your lack of insurance coverage. You should not expect to play your senior year."

My mind refused to process what I was hearing. How could I miss my senior year? How would I get to college? My life was over. It all felt so unfair. I had followed the rules, stayed out of trouble, done well enough academically. But it had not been enough. Bad luck had ruined my prospects. The bullets had missed me, but a stray hit had taken everything away. A lifetime of training and focus had not helped me overcome a poorly timed jump from my teammate.

That night I prayed to God: *I've read stories of miracles in the Bible. You restored sight to the blind, cleansed lepers of illness, and raised the dead. Surely you won't leave me with a useless knee and broken dreams. You know how hard I worked. I tried to do everything right, stayed away from drugs. I was in church nearly every Sunday. You owe me. I can't end like this.*

I shifted my legs from the bed onto the floor and reached for my crutches to get myself on my feet. But then, in an act of faith, I set them aside. I heaved myself up and tried to walk without the crutches to support me, sure that God would knit my ligaments back together. There was no miracle. My knee buckled and I fell to the ground, much like I had the night I was injured. I lay there weeping.

As providence would have it, the year I got hurt was the same year my mother had convinced me to take my first AP class for college credit. The subject was U.S. history, and the instructor, Mrs. Bailey, was one of those idealistic teachers whose love for the subject couldn't help but pique the curiosity of even the most stubborn student. During the first semester I enjoyed her class so much that I found myself attending the extra study sessions she offered to help us prepare for the national exam. Now I had little else to do, so I began to make flash cards that included key dates and historical figures. I took the practice tests and got accustomed to sketching out essays and writing on a time limit. I found that I liked the process more than I'd realized. The test took place toward the end of the school year, with the results coming directly to the teacher.

That spring day, I found myself gathered with a bunch of other students in Mrs. Bailey's classroom to hear how we had done. No local paper would record the performances of our little class of budding historians, but student after student celebrated as they received the news that they had done well enough to receive college credit. For most of them, being near the top of the seniors' graduating class, this was expected. This could not be said for me, a football player sneaked in by his mother's politicking. Maybe that was why Mrs. Bailey made a show of giving me my grade. She handed me a sheet of paper and, after I had read the results, said, "That's right, you are a junior in high school and you already have college credit. You can be whatever you want to be."

Her words weren't any different from the speeches my mother had given me a thousand times, but that exam convinced me that I could indeed find another path to college. I might not have been a star athlete anymore, but if I studied for the rest of my classes the way I'd studied for that AP exam, I could pull my grades up enough to get to college another way—my mom's way.

For the rest of that semester and the following one, there wasn't a study session I didn't attend or an extra-credit opportunity I let pass. The B's and C's on my report cards were replaced by A's.

At first, no one seemed to care. The calls from coaches and letters from major universities had stopped after my injury. It was as if the athletic world got a memo announcing that I was damaged goods. This motivated me to study even harder. It also changed the way I viewed sports. I realized that those coaches who'd given up on me did not care about me as a person. They were only concerned with what I had to offer the sport. Once I couldn't further their objectives for the team, their interest in me came to an end.

I became determined to prove them wrong—but not in the sense of coming back to some starring role on a football field. I wanted to show that my Black life didn't depend on the strength of my knee. I was more than a Black body, useful only when I collided with other desperate boys wrestling for control of the football. I had a Black mind.

I still wanted to play football the following year, but there was the problem of insurance. We could not afford the surgery needed to repair my knee. My mom prayed for a miracle of her own, though her prayers were more practical than my bedroom plea for immediate healing: *God, please find my son a surgeon.* She knew the right type of miracle to ask for, one that allowed the story to continue, even if dramatically changed. I had not yet learned that lesson.

It seemed God was predisposed to heed my mother's request, because a doctor soon appeared. A few weeks after my diagnosis, my mom got a call. The doctor who'd examined my knee had seen me play football and thought I had a chance to be special. He volunteered to do the surgery for free. He also arranged for me to receive free physical therapy for as long as I needed it.

For the eight months following the surgery, I drove across town to the rich part of Huntsville and received the best medical care money could provide. Where the workout manual had once saved me, now it was the rehab routine. Whatever exercises I was told to do, I doubled the repetitions. As I sat at our kitchen tabling puzzling over math problems or writing history essays, I'd clench my thigh muscle over and over to strengthen the supporting structures around my knee. As I lay in bed at night, I'd do leg raises until I fell asleep.

I would never regain the speed and agility I had before the injury, but when the time came for the first day of practice my senior year, I was cleared for all football-related activities after only eight months, far ahead of the original timeline. After being told that I'd miss the season, I didn't miss even a single day of practice.

There would be no full return to glory. McCaulley family stories do not work like that. By the time the season ended, I was no longer a Division I-A recruit. Offers came in from

Division I-AA and Division II schools, but knowing how quickly football could disappear, I was hesitant to accept them. If I got hurt again, would I lose my scholarship? The coaches told me that if I did get hurt again, they would take care of me, but having learned from my father the danger of trusting in the promises made by men, I demurred.

As I wrestled with what to do, a coach reached out to see if I was interested in playing football for the University of the South. He hadn't heard about me during the peak of my athletic abilities, since any player being recruited by a Division I school is unlikely to return a Division III coach's call. But my slide into Division II had put me on his radar. A few games into my senior year, the recruiter had come to a game at Johnson High. He'd asked my coach for my contact information, and a few weeks later, he'd called. Since Division III schools don't give athletic scholarships, he explained, I would need to get accepted on my academic merits, but need-based financial aid would cover most of my tuition.

The recruiter was honest in saying that my grades made my prospects a little iffy. Sewanee, as the University of the South is commonly known, was ranked in the top twenty-five liberal arts schools in the country at the time. However, I'd maintained a 4.0 GPA since the second half of my junior year, and the recruiter thought that should be enough to get me in. It was. I was accepted into the University of the South. I became a student athlete, but no coach would control my destiny. I had earned my spot.

I have often thought about the two prayers that surrounded that injury, both concerning my future. One came from me, the other from my mother. I prayed that God would work an immediate miracle and get me back to the football field. My mother's prayer was different. Knowing that my dream had died the Friday night of my injury, she prayed for God to make a way through to the other side. She asked God to be there amid my suffering, not to remove it from me. She knew that there are no easy escapes in life; sometimes the miracle is God-given strength.

The morning I left for college, I sat with my family, eating off-brand Froot Loops as the news played in the background. It was a joyous day. My older sister, Latasha, was two years into becoming the first member of our family to earn a bachelor's degree. If all went well, four years later I would become the second.

I was feeling good about my life when the face of my friend Jesse appeared on the TV screen. He had been murdered in a random act of gun violence the night before.

Jesse was a flashy kid who always dressed nicely but never used what he had to make you feel like you were less than him. He had a great sense of humor and a slight hitch in his voice that made everything he said seem a bit funnier. Jesse's mom, Betty, was a fixture at Johnson High School—not a volunteer like my mom but a substitute teacher. Jesse was her only child; she showered him with clothes and bought him a nice car. Betty had done everything right, like my own mom had. And so had Jesse. Weeks earlier, at the height of the summer, I'd run into him at the Black arts festival, and we'd chatted for a few minutes. I would be going to Sewanee and he would be attending Middle Tennessee State, about an hour away.

Before we parted ways, I said, "We should connect sometime in Tennessee."

He said, "Bet."

Now I would be leaving for college; he would not.

As the sugary colored cereal bled into the milk, I contemplated the magnitude of what lay before me. I was not going to college for me. I was going to college for those whose stories had ended without a proper resolution, who wouldn't get the chance to test the limits of their abilities. I would succeed, and I would remember Jesse. I would remember the whole of it. I wouldn't lie about the world that created the dynamics I had to endure, about how some of us broke and some survived.

CHAPTER 5

Survival Is Complicated

In Huntsville, Blackness had been so normal that I didn't realize the full impact of living in a Black world until I arrived at Sewanee. I had spent time in the white part of Huntsville, but only as a visitor; it had never been home. There was no "white part" of Sewanee. It encompassed the whole of the campus and the surrounding community.

The coach who recruited me had boasted about the school's academic rankings. "By the time you graduate," he'd said, "your brain will be worth almost a quarter of a million dollars."

Impressed with that figure, I had not considered the cost of the cultural shift.

The University of the South sits on top of the Cumberland Plateau—referred to as "the Mountain" by locals—forty-five minutes outside of Chattanooga; the campus is known for its Gothic-style sandstone and granite buildings. The stately architecture suggested that this place held all that college was meant to provide: a chance to learn and develop while surrounded by splendor. To remind myself of home, I'd brought along my high school football jersey, a collection of CDs, and, at my mom's insistence, a picture of Black Jesus teaching caramel-colored disciples beside the Sea of Galilee. Because the football players arrived before everyone else, the campus was occupied only by residential staffers, athletes, and international students who lived in the dorms year-round.

Located on the outskirts of the college, my residence hall, a brown limestone building with an open area in the middle, was an inconvenient fifteen-minute walk from the center of campus. From the outside, as I approached, it looked perfect, nestled between a pair of matching lakes, but the concrete interior reminded me of the housing projects I'd visited as a kid, and the walls would remain mostly bare, since damage in the form of nail holes would result in a fine.

I had been assigned a room on the second floor. As I made my way upstairs, the sticky summer heat seemed to follow me, and I noticed that a few doors had been left open by students hoping to catch a breeze; there was no air-conditioning. Balancing a box in my arms, I glanced into a couple of rooms as I passed, then stopped transfixed at a room where a Confederate flag hung from a large section of blank wall. Few images are lodged as deeply in the Black imagination as that blue-and-white X with thirteen stars inside it. Seeing that flag in a place I viewed as an entryway to the land of opportunity caused my body to go stiff and my heart to race. Up to that point, the only Confederate flags I'd seen had been the ones waving from the backs of pickup trucks on Alabama roadways, indicating that I'd taken a wrong turn. This one seemed to suggest the same thing here.

Time slowed as I paused in the doorframe. It was clear that my hallmate had not considered how a Black person might feel upon seeing his flag displayed. When our eyes met, it was not shame I saw on his face but an expression of discomfort mingled with a forced sense of pride. There were no words to bridge the divide between us. That gap widened as I continued my journey down the hall to my room.

That moment would remain with me as a reminder of the fresh trials I would face in Sewanee. Life in Northwest Huntsville had taught me how to survive, to tell by the set of a person's jaw or the coldness in their eye whether they were a friend or a threat. And my mom's endless attempts to get me to take schooling seriously had instilled in me a sense of self and dignity. All those lessons had helped me navigate my community and make it to Sewanee, but what about Black life now at a nearly all-white university that still clung to remnants of the Confederacy?

I had arrived at Sewanee on a full scholarship, but I would come to find that many students' families were able to pay the full tuition, or close to it. Having that much money was so far outside my experience as to be inconceivable. But money wasn't always evident in how my fellow students dressed; as I'd soon learn, the same people who wore clothes from charity shops drove Rangers Rovers and Lexuses around the Mountain because money meant *not having to care* about your appearance. The week before spring break, I was sitting around a lunch table with a group of classmates when they asked me about my plans. Since my itinerary didn't consist of much beyond driving the one hour back to Huntsville, I didn't elaborate; they then went on to describe their own plans to travel to the Caribbean and Europe. I never quite mastered what to say when people talked of family vacations at ski resorts and summers spent at beach homes. Was I to counter with the memory of my visit to Opryland one year or how I'd considered myself fortunate to partake in a day trip to Six Flags Over Georgia?

And how could we talk about the things that really mattered? Ideological divisions on campus did not run the range from Black pessimism to Black nationalism, from a disengaged Black church to an engaged one, the way they did in my neighborhood. From what I could tell, Sewanee's spectrum ran from white conservatives to white liberals. The latter wanted the whole of the South to be more like Austin, Texas. They were the ones who had read all the Black books and knew what we needed without actually knowing any Black people. They slid bell hooks and Toni Morrison quotes into normal conversation and complained that Rush Limbaugh had ruined the country. I also sometimes ran into straitlaced conservatives. They told me that I really needed to read Thomas Sowell and learn that the Democratic Party really didn't care about Black people. All true Christians, I was told, were fiscal conservatives and strict constructivists. Then there were the few blatant racists, who excluded Black students from their social gatherings and wrapped themselves in the lore of the Confederacy. We knew who they were and where they hung out, and we made no real attempt to engage or change them. We and they lived side by side, trying to avoid unnecessary conflicts.

Out-and-out racists aside, my place on the periphery of the school would become most evident to me in the college's robust fraternity life. Parties took place at a dozen or so frat houses, all of them historically white. Fraternities were a strange mix of people interested in community service, those who wanted an intentional friend group on campus, and folks who threw parties. Different frats had more of one thing or another, but most tended to place a heavy emphasis on having a good time come the weekend. To my knowledge, some had never had a Black pledge.

One of my best friends on campus was a Black first-year football player like me, a guy named Devin. Also like me, he'd grown up in poverty and had never had a relationship with his father. He'd been recruited as a running back; I, a linebacker. Our first day in practice, when the coaches paired us up in tackling drills, he was eager to show his toughness by running over the star defensive player, while I was keen to put the standout runner in his place. I must admit that our battle was pretty even, with him putting a spin move on me in the first rep and me tackling him immediately in the second. It went on that way throughout much of the rest of our time at Sewanee. But competition done with integrity breeds friendship, so Devin and I became close. Two young Black men trying to make it in a white world.

During rush week, Devin and I talked about which frats

were most likely to welcome us. First to be crossed off our lists were the fraternities that flew Confederate flags. We went to a few interviews and reconvened to compare notes:

What was it like?

The vibe was off. You know what I mean?

Yes! They said, "We are just trying to determine whether you would be a good fit." I looked at them and then I looked at myself and wondered what I could say that would make me "fit." They asked me about my background and interests and how they lined up with the fraternity's mission. They had all clearly come from money, and nothing in their mission had anything to do with Black people.

In time, the Black students would find each other and co-alesce into a community. But I spent most of my first year in my room. Needing to show that I was not some charity case, admitted only because I played football, I stayed up late writing and rewriting papers, determined to prove to myself that these wealthy white students were not better than me.

In my spare time, I initiated protests to revise the university's admissions procedures, questioning why the student body of thirteen hundred included only some two dozen African American students. Why was there only one Black faculty member in the humanities? I joined with my fellow Black students to push for a more diverse faculty. When I read Cornel West's *Race Matters,* I was so moved that I organized a campus-wide event to address racism. I was elected president of the African American Alliance, the Black student group on campus. When Black fraternities refused to establish a chapter at Sewanee, we started our own local fraternity, as a place of refuge and cultural affirmation. My papers hummed with a barely contained fury at the old injustices that I'd read about in books and the fresh ones I experienced as I carried this Black skin into and out of the local grocery stores, restaurants, and gas stations of the tiny towns surrounding the campus.

But in all the fighting and pushing for this right and that new agenda, I lost myself.

Despite my abhorrence for white culture as symbolized by the Confederate flag, I began to adopt a set of white postures and intellectual habits. If my options were Austin, Texas, or the South envisioned by Rush Limbaugh, I chose the former. Austin and I, after all, shared a disdain for the anti-Black policies and habits of extreme conservatism. Yet although we shared a commitment to fight racism, in other ways there were real differences.

Those differences included divergent religious habits. My liberal friends and I often saw God differently. They told me that the faith of my ancestors was an opiate keeping me from liberation. It had been useful in overcoming my childhood environment, but God wasn't needed anymore. European thought and a sufficiently radical form of democratic socialism would take it from here.

Like the college students I now teach, I adopted the philosophical and political ideas I'd first heard as a freshman and dismissed anyone who didn't share my newly formed views as lacking enlightenment. I had a good friend on the football team named Chris. He played offensive line and was a bit slow of foot. In practice, I often ran by him or over him on the way to the quarterback. But he handled it all well, and we were friendly on campus. Once, when we were walking out of the cafeteria, he took a risk and asked me if I wanted to go to Bible study. I could see the nervousness in his eyes and his need to be accepted. Even so, I didn't care. I said, "Nope" and walked away.

It was a small thing, but I remember being pleased with myself for acting so cold and casually dismissive. *Forget his feelings,* I told myself.

If I'd arrived at Sewanee with the goal of building a résumé that would secure a stable future, it would be difficult to call my first three years anything but successful. I won awards for leadership and intellectual achievements. Graduate school was in my sights if I desired it. Having branched out from my Black social circles, I even tolerated the folk-rockers who filled the fraternity houses on Friday and Saturday nights. I had to admit that a few songs by the Eagles and Fleetwood Mac were passable.

Still, despite all I'd achieved, I couldn't shake this feeling that might be best summed up with a shoulder shrug. For all my talk of rebellion, I had been formed into exactly what some at Sewanee wanted me to be: a Black intellectual who took the progressive side in all-white conversations about politics and theology. Stated differently, my professors and classmates wanted Black people to call out racism and critique the system, and that was about it. They needed Black voices to challenge their enemies on the right; they needed their critiques dipped in chocolate. That was our role on campus. Even my rebellion felt scripted. I needed to find a distinctively Black and Christian way of being. I needed less Bertrand Russell and more Frederick Douglass. I needed the space to access the unfiltered voices of Black people who came before me.

When I returned home for Christmas my junior year, my aunties and cousins greeted me as the hometown boy who'd escaped and made a name for himself, not knowing that I was mired in internal conflict. Having never been to the Mountain, how could my family understand my doubts about my future and what I was gaining and losing on campus?

In my absence, my former bedroom had been claimed by my younger sister, Marketha, and I was relegated to the room formerly inhabited by her and Latasha. I locked myself in, pulled the drapery closed, and lay across the bed, the rose-petal bedspread and soft yellow walls posing a stark contradiction to my mood. Sleep fled as I listened to the jazz music my grandfather had taught me to love, the various events of the last few years competing for my attention. Something was missing, or maybe everything was missing. All those things that had kept me busy, running from classroom to football field to protest and back again, had served another unseen purpose. They had distracted me from the more pressing question of who I was. Who was the person hiding underneath all the striving? What was I building or becoming other than a series of actions dedicated to a vaguely defined concept of good? I pondered these things as I lay in the dark atop my sister's bed, listening to Etta James sing that her whole world had gone misty blue.

In that moment, the most piercing of questions imposed itself upon me. It was not a voice but an idea—a question that wrote itself into my soul, a place from which it has never escaped: *What do you do when you have everything you ever wanted, but it is not sufficient to bring you joy?* An answer etched itself right next to the question, the completion of a thought that arose from elsewhere, more a request than a demand: *Consider Jesus.* I saw then that all the things that had marked my first three years of college weren't evil; they simply were not a life. A life needs a *telos:* a picture of the good, the true, and the beautiful compelling enough to give order to the varied parts of the human experience. The life of Christ had previously captured my imagination, much as it had done for my antebellum ancestors when they gathered covertly, believing God to be the sole hope of the disinherited. At some point during my sojourn at Sewanee, I had set aside that hope passed down to me through the generations. It was time to take it up again, but with nuances born of my time on the Mountain.

Sewanee had given me the intellectual tools to speak about structural racism and the detrimental impact it had on Black life—something that previously I could intuit but hadn't yet been able to pen into sentences and paragraphs. The university had gifted me with the ability to articulate the overlapping causes of poverty that keep people trapped in the underclass. I was grateful for all that, even if much of that analysis was *about* my community instead of *from* my community.

I had been poor, and I had experienced racism. There was another problem missing from the analysis. It wasn't simply that people out there had done wrong; I had done wrong. I had harmed others, and other poor people had harmed me.

The disheveled masses weren't always noble. We could be as callous as the wealthy.

I didn't need to be told that society had failed Black people, nor did I need to know that my father had mistreated me. I needed the spiritual resources to forgive or at least to become more than the jumble of grievances I had collected during my twenty-one years on the planet. I didn't yet have a full understanding of what all this might mean, but that was the beginning of the search for a positive vision of my life that included more than being different from my father.

Part II

THE VINE AND FIG TREE

CHAPTER 6

Sophia's Gift

If every family has a point of origin or turn, my father's family's began with Sophia. Born in a small town in rural Alabama in 1901, my father's grandmother is remembered as both a heroic and a tragic figure, someone who should have seen more fruit from her labor. The oldest of five children, Sophia is said to have been the smartest, the most quick-witted of the bunch. But at the time, few thought it worth the effort to educate a Black woman. To the end of her life, she signed her name with an X, a mark indistinguishable from those left by countless other Black folks deprived of the opportunity to learn to read.

Sophia was a dreamer of dreams and seer of visions. Born with the gift of prophecy, she could tell you whether the long-hoped-for job opportunity would come to pass. She had the ability to predict pregnancies and the success or failure of potential relationships. According to family lore, Sophia's power came from the veil that covered her face as a newborn. This thin, clear membrane, known as a caul, appears in one of roughly eighty thousand births when a bit of amniotic sac attaches itself to the newborn's face. I do not believe that Sophia's special powers arose from the veil, but I don't doubt her gift or the weight it carried in my father's family. They respected it yet also made light of it, often stating, with a hint of laughter, when the outcome of her prediction was in doubt, "This time your prophecy will fail."

When my mother became pregnant again after having me, Sophia told her she would have a daughter. My mom, having just gone for an ultrasound, laughed like the others. "Your powers must have failed you this time," she told Sophia, "because they say it's a boy." She did not yet know that tragedy would prove the accuracy of Sophia's declaration.

Four months into my mother's pregnancy, my father came home to our trailer drunk. Alcohol made him irritable, and this led to a fight about his increasingly worrying habits. According to my mother, she rushed toward the door, planning to spend the night with Wavon and Sophia up in the big house, but when my father reached out to pull her back, she jerked away and fell down the porch steps. As she hit the ground, she screamed in pain. "I felt a lump come out of me," she later told me. "I knew I had lost the child. I went to the doctor, who confirmed that I had miscarried. It was a boy."

A follow-up ultrasound revealed that my mother had been carrying twins. A second child's heart still beat in her womb. My younger sister, Marketha, had survived the fall. And so five months later, my mother gave birth to a daugther, just as Sophia had predicted.

Like many Black folks in rural Alabama, my great-grandmother worked as a tenant farmer. It gets hot every-where, but Alabama seems to have done something to earn the sun's ire, its fervent heat reserved for the heart of the Confederacy. Visitors unaccustomed to Alabama's summer sun are often surprised to encounter a searing glare that makes them dizzy. The sun tanned Sophia's skin and pulled the sweat from her pores as she picked cotton on white-owned farms all around Alabama and Tennessee. After a long day in the fields, she spent her evenings cleaning houses. She swept hardwood floors and made the designs of flower petals and candles on stained-glass windows glisten. She scrubbed bathrooms so that they would not betray signs of use, shielding the wealthy from the grime common to hu-manity. In addition to cleaning houses and picking cotton, Sophia also moonlighted as a midwife. She learned how to birth babies from other Black women who had guided hun-dreds of ebony infants into the world.

When Sophia had trouble with a birth, she would ask God for help. When Wavon was pregnant with my father, Sophia discovered that the child had turned the wrong way in her daughter's womb. Having never delivered a breech baby, and knowing a broken neck to be a real risk, she prayed to the Lord for assistance. She credited the Holy Spirit for guiding her hands, and my father was born without injury.

With the money she earned from farming, cleaning houses, and practicing midwifery, Sophia saved up to buy a small plot of land from one of her employers, whom she referred to as Mr. Anderson. Located about twenty minutes outside Huntsville in an area known as "the country," the one-and-a-half-acre parcel was situated on a slight incline that made farming difficult, with a gravel road dividing the plot in half. It sat next to other bits and pieces owned by the Andersons and other white families, all of the area criss-crossed by dirt roads, muddy streams, and rough terrain. Sophia believed that the Andersons sold it to her in part because of the poor quality of the soil, but for her the land felt like paradise. In the words of the biblical prophets, she had her own "vine and fig tree," a little bit of happiness.

Midway through saving for a place of her own, Sophia married Bud. How they met is lost to family history. No one knows what promises he made or what future they planned together. We do not know if they met in the fields picking cotton or if they cleaned homes side by side. We only know that Bud left behind a legacy of abuse and wrongs done to Sophia. Every payday, he came home and beat Sophia for her money, leaving her bloodied and bruised while he went to the juke joints and run-down clubs of backwoods Alabama. He used her money to keep more than one mistress well stocked with food and fancy clothes. He spread the pain around, beating those women, too, and leaving them with children to raise alone.

Sometimes if what we do is sufficiently dark, the space for nuance is left behind. We become the evil we did in the hearts and minds of those who remember us. In my family's recollections, Bud is known without context, only through his sins.

Bud was, in part, a product of his times. Jim Crow pressed its knee on the necks of Black men all over the South. These men knew their options would be limited by the whims of a power structure that denied them fair access to education, housing, and pay. These men were addressed as "boy" or "son" regardless of their age, disrespected in front of their wives and children in private and in public. Did those everyday traumas cause men like Bud to seek freedom from the responsibility to love and provide? Did racist insults stir up rage inside him until he could not help but release it onto those closest to him? Did this same feeling of rage and frustration cause my own father to flee? Maybe. But evil cannot be wholly explained by the brokenness of the world. Sometimes we participate in the breaking.

Sophia sought refuge in her faith. She couldn't read the Bible, but she heard scripture in church every Sunday. At home, she clutched a Bible in her hands and prayed long after the sun had set, with the night stars shining bright while most everyone else slept. Sophia talked to God the way a person might converse with a close friend. She called on him to keep his promises in the same informal English that she used to scold her unruly children.

The evidence of her trauma would have been plain in her bruises. She came into church with a large brood of kids, wearing her best sundress along with extra makeup to cover her injuries. The stiffness in her gait bore witness to the dull pain that lingered in various parts of her body.

When the pastor could no longer ignore her wounds or pretend that her explanations of how she'd gotten them made any sense, he took her aside after church. "God wants more for you, Sophia," he said. "There is a freedom on the other side if you want to leave Bud. We can help."

Sophia couldn't bring herself to break free. She and Bud had seven children together. Rather than considering what she lost by staying in the relationship, she thought about what her husband contributed. He worked from time to time and helped with a few of the bills. Without that money, she couldn't make it.

Every person has a breaking point, and there was nothing particularly special about the day when Sophia ultimately reached hers. As was his habit, Bud came home on payday and began looking through the cupboards and under beds for the money she had stashed away. When she refused to give up her hiding places, he hit her, as usual, then left to grab a beer. But that day, as she lay on the living room floor, she felt something in her snap. Bud returned to find her standing up, a shotgun pointed at his head.

Seeing the determination in her eyes, he dropped to his knees to plead for his life. But it was too late. "I am going to kill you for what you've been doing to me," Sophia explained, without a trace of uncertainty.

Reaching for the trigger, Sophia heard a voice. *Do you love me?*

Thinking it was Bud, Sophia said, "No, I don't love you. I hate you."

Then she realized it was God talking to her. *Yes, I love you,* she told God.

God replied: *Then let him go.*

Sophia lowered her gun. "God has told me not to kill

you," she explained, "and right now, I am listening to him. But I cannot guarantee that I will keep listening. Get your stuff and get out. If I see you again, you are a dead man."

Bud got up and fled. The family never saw him again.

Anyone would have felt sympathy for Sophia had she pulled that trigger. But she probably would have gone to jail, leaving her children scattered to the wind. Divine intervention kept my great-grandmother from becoming a killer; now she would raise her children on her own in an uncertain future. My family story, I think, turns on that moment, an instance of undeserved mercy that allowed her and us to move forward. For that I am grateful.

Sophia would do just fine without Bud. Absent her husband's thefts, her work as a midwife and a housekeeper proved enough to pay the bills. Most of her children left home as they came of age, finding jobs as farmers and cleaners, and joining the lower-class workforce open to rural Black folks. But my grandmother Wavon had always been something of a momma's girl. When Sophia got too old to work, Wavon stayed home to take care of her and took over her cleaning jobs to pay the bills. Noticing her hard work and mental aptitude, Dr. Mccinlish, whose medical office she cleaned, decided to teach her basic nursing skills. Soon she was putting in IVs and giving shots and able to leave cleaning behind.

It was progress, small and steady. Wavon even managed to make a better choice in marriage when she wed my grandfather Gus. Like Wavon, Gus could not read, but he was a religious man, and he did not drink. On Sundays, he wore his best pair of overalls and a starched white shirt to church, and according to my grandmother, he had a kind word and an open smile for every member of the congregation. During the week, he drove the bus that ferried colored students to and from the segregated schools in the area.

Recognizing his piety and his solid reputation, the church appointed Gus as a deacon. (Huntsville's Union Hill Primitive Baptist Church, a traditional all-Black congregation, consisted of fewer than one hundred souls back then. When my mother joined, decades later, it had grown to some twelve hundred members. It was the same church where I would deliver my father's eulogy.)

Gus loved Wavon well at the beginning. When they met, she had two children by other men (a minor scandal during this era), but this did not frighten him away. He counted them as his own and never treated them differently. He worked as hard as Wavon and earned extra money by taking on cleaning jobs in the evenings. Together, they made more than enough to take care of Sophia in her old age, buy nice clothes, and feed their six kids. They even drove a fancy car, a red-and-blue Chevrolet Bel Air that was the talk of the neighborhood. The early years of their marriage were the picture of Black possibility, even in the Jim Crow South. Disrespected and limited in the white world, they carved out a little bit of happiness in the Black one. It seemed to Sophia that her daughter had pulled together that pristine family life in the promised land of her dreams. Sophia might not have experienced such a life herself, but she could watch her daughter and son-in-law enjoy it together.

Gus and Wavon's life went along smoothly until the chilly

winter of 1956. Most Alabama winters are mild affairs, making gloves and knit hats a rare necessity. But the insides of any home can feel frosty when the sun sinks below the hills. Arriving home late from work, Gus threw some kindling in the fireplace, thinking he'd warm the house. To jump-start it, he then poured a little oil over the wood and lit a match, not knowing that earlier in the evening Wavon had started a fire. The warm embers still lurked beneath the ashes, invisible to Gus's tired eyes on a dark night. When the match hit the kindling, a blaze erupted from the fireplace and set the surrounding wall aflame. There was no fire alarm in the house, so Gus had to dash from room to room, alerting everyone in the family to the danger.

The two youngest boys, two-year-old twins, were sleeping in the room nearest to where the fire began. But the flames barred Gus's entrance. Despite his valiant attempts to save them, he could not rescue the pair, who died silently in their beds.

Gus's repeated forays into the house led to burns that covered more than 25 percent of his body and would require extended care inside a Birmingham hospital. His body healed, but he was never the same husband or father after the loss of his two sons. How could he be?

At first, no one in the family knew how the fire had started, given the chaos of that night. When they came to pick Gus up from the hospital, he wept and told them that he had failed them all. None of their attempts at comfort could convince him otherwise. The pain of that night would wrap the family in silence. I would not learn the full details until Auntie Sweetie, the oldest of Gus and Wavon's surviving children, informed me of Gus's role in the fire during the writing of this book.

My father, Esau Sr., and his younger brother, Steven (whom everyone called Barney), were born a few years after the fire, bringing the total number of living children back to six. They grew up in the shadows of those flames; whatever mistakes they made were always set against the potential of the two young boys who had perished in the fire.

Those boys never caused no problems.

They were talking and walking at an early age.

They were both as smart as whips.

And they were cute. You knew they were going to grow into something.

In contrast, Esau and Steve were seen as wild, troublesome, and cold—unable to meet the standards set by their parents.

As a kid, I saw something approaching shame in my father's eyes, a deep embarrassment that he couldn't quite shake. I don't know if it had to do with his two dead brothers, my mother's miscarriage, or something else. But I remember that he seemed to love Marketha more intensely than the rest of us, showering her with extra gifts one moment and hostility the next. My mom tells me, "Sometimes when your father got drunk, he didn't get angry, he got sad. He would just go to crying and crying like a baby about that child. He would say that he was sorry, and I would just hold him until he stopped heaving."

In an attempt to move on toward a better future, Gus convinced Wavon and Sophia to take out a loan from the

Anderson family so that the house could be rebuilt. The new shotgun house, a white cinder-block structure with four bedrooms all shooting off from a single hallway, inherited the name "the big house" from the home that burned to the ground.

No one in the family knew the terms of the loan, except Wavon and Gus. What we do know is that neither of them could read what they signed. We also know that Wavon took monthly payments to the Andersons from 1956 or '57 until her death in 2006. After her death, the land that should have been inherited by my father and his siblings reverted back to the Andersons. Instead of allowing generational wealth to be passed down through our family, the Andersons received a monthly check for five decades, long enough to pay back the loan, and then reclaimed that land for themselves. Sometimes I think about buying back that land, as a redemption of sorts, but first I would need to find out if it is already legally ours by right. The skeleton of Gus and Wavon's house, I am told, is still there.

In any case, fixing the house did not restore what the fire had destroyed. Unable to forgive himself, Gus sought comfort in drinking and other women, the same refuge sought a generation later by his son. He began to disappear for months at a time, and the family would hear word of him shacking up with women in the next town and as far away as New York. By 1970, when Gus brought a white girlfriend home to meet his wife and remaining children, Wavon had reached her limit. She pulled a gun on him, as her mother had done with her abuser, only Wavon didn't just threaten. She shot at him. She missed, according to familial consensus, on purpose. Gus fled to New York City, leaving Wavon behind to care for the six children still living on the property, ranging in age from eight to twenty-eight.

In the fall of 1975, Gus returned for the last time. Now alone, he explained to Wavon that he had come home to die. Nodding solemnly, she took him in.

Gus's return would not be seen as cause for celebration; he would not be greeted with tear-filled hugs from his children. Instead, he came home tired, wanting to spend the last days of his life in the only place that felt like home, a place where he had experienced his greatest joys and his deepest sorrows. He died a few months after his return. The last thing he said to Wavon was that those two boys, Steven and Esau, would be the death of her. Soon after that, at the age of seventeen, my dad met my mother.

How does one love and provide in a system designed to make that nearly impossible? When I learned my family history for the first time, that was the question that lingered with me.

Sophia was a hero in our family because she overcame abuse, tragedy, financial exploitation, and naked racism. My father was a villain because he deserted us when we needed him. But even in the realm of childhood fantasy, monsters and heroes are not just born. They are made. The same trauma that sets the context for heroic bravery also creates the possibility for failure.

It took me a long time to see this, and to find the grace and the forgiveness that come with understanding. The extent of Sophia's efforts and the depths of the familial trauma my father experienced confirmed a suspicion that had been growing within me over the course of my entire life. It was not enough for me merely to survive, nor could I accept partial truths about the people whose lives shaped mine. I had to find beauty. I had to see something in the struggle itself that was worthy of remembering and carrying forward. That was Sophia's gift to me. She showed me that a Black life could be lived with honor through faith, even when the world was set against you. I would need to do something with this gift.

CHAPTER 7

Running from the South

In the spring of 1992, the year I turned thirteen, I came home from school one afternoon to find my mother troubled. She called me over to our living room, to the brown-and-white floral-patterned couch, a holdover from the 1970s, bought on the cheap from Goodwill when she couldn't afford new furniture. Sitting on the couch and talking was normal. But to be *called to the couch* meant that a rebuke or a life lesson was coming, or at least that something out of the ordinary had occurred. I sat reluctantly.

Her voice took on the professional tone I recognized from her phone conversations with white people. "You probably saw the news about Rodney King."

I had. All the kids had been talking about it in class.

"I am going to tell you how to avoid that happening to you," she continued, addressing not the twelve-year-old on the couch but, instead, the future driver. Her aim wasn't to educate me about right or wrong; it was to instruct me about the best way to stay alive. She held up a finger to punctuate each command:

Rule 1: Never speed.

Rule 2: Don't switch lanes without putting on your signal.

Rule 3: Make sure your brake lights work before you get in the car.

Rule 4: If they pull you over, *do what they ask,* even if they have no legal right to make the request.

Rule 5: *Do not lose your temper. Do not raise your voice.*

Rule 6: Do not make any quick movements.

Rule 7: Be respectful. Answer every question with "sir" or "ma'am."

Rule 8: If you can, avoid getting out of the car.

Rule 9: Do not drive through rural or known racist places at night.

When she finished laying out the rules, the mock-white professionalism in her voice slipped away and the southern drawl distinctive of Black city folks returned. She looked tired. She let out a long sigh and slumped her shoulders, having finished her long-dreaded task.

I tried to comfort her. "It'll be fine, Mom. I won't get into any trouble."

She laughed a bit. "It's not you I'm worried about."

The aftermath of the King incident was not the only time my mother would give me the talk. I heard it with more consistency as I grew into my adult body. Sometimes the advice focused on what to do while driving; other times it concerned how to function in all-white spaces or when confronted by an authority figure. I would learn from her that Black bodies can be seen as dangerous when driving or simply walking around. By the time I turned sixteen and got my license, my flimsy mustache had morphed into a full beard and my voice had dropped an octave. She said, "Remember what I told you. You follow my rules in them streets. And get home. Nothing good happens after midnight."

I would have plenty of opportunities to put her rules to use, but I will limit myself to six accounts of what it was like to exist in this Black body in Alabama. Each incident occurred without warning as I was going about the ordinary tasks of life. Not even my mother's carefully thought-through lectures could have prepared me for being Black in Alabama.

Two Trips to the Mall

The spot for teens in 1990s Huntsville was Madison Square Mall. Everything teenage boys needed to start the weekend was there: the food court, friends, and the chance to meet girls. Knowing this, mall security instituted a rule against gathering in crowds or standing in one place. Shoppers or strollers needed to be in constant motion. My friends Brandon and Corey and I dipped in and out of clothing and shoe stores, killing time until the movie we had purchased tickets for began.

I was feeling good because I had worked up the nerve to ask a girl for her phone number and, much to my surprise, she had written it down for me. Brandon and Corey gave me a hard time as we walked across the parking lot to the theater.

"Man, I bet you that's the wrong number."

"No, she made me repeat it to be sure I had it down."

"What school did she say she went to?"

"Sparkman. That's way out in Harvest somewhere, right?"

"What was she doing here?"

"She came hoping to meet somebody like me."

I said that last part with more confidence than I felt. Brandon and Corey had no fear when it came to girls, but I was much more shy and clumsy.

We were so involved in our conversation that we didn't notice the security guard, an older white man who apparently took his job of watchman seriously, driving up alongside us. "You boys doing okay this evening?" he asked, with more than a little hostility in his voice.

We knew that a mall cop was not an agent of the state—more likely, an hourly wage worker making extra money on the weekend. And yet my mother's advice held. I replied, "We're doing fine, sir."

"Where y'all heading?"

The bright sign that read "Movie Theater" lit up the night, making it clear where we were heading. Brandon told him anyway, but the guard wasn't satisfied. Turning his head to me, he asked, "Is that true, son? What movie you going to see? When is the start time?"

I chuckled to myself, deciding to ignore his use of the word *son*. Corey, however, responded with the same hostile energy that guard had given us: "You are a mall cop. We don't have to listen to you."

My heart sped as I recalled one of my mother's rules: *Do whatever they ask*. Inherent in that rule was another one—*Do not lose your temper*—and Corey had already lost his.

The guard stared at us for an uncomfortably long time, clearly considering an escalation. I could hear snatches of conversations taking place nearby. As his silence continued, my adrenaline pulsed. Finally, he moved on to another group of kids.

This encounter with mall security stood in stark contrast to one I'd had when I was in the fourth grade, about six years earlier. It was near Christmastime, and my mother had taken me to the mall to get some shoes. I was hoping to have a new pair of Nikes to start the next semester in style.

In the middle of our shopping trip, she ran into one of the ladies from church and started talking. Bored, I wandered out of the store they were in and into Foot Locker, trying to find some kicks that wouldn't get me bullied.

My mother must not have seen me go, because when I returned, she was nowhere to be found. As I rushed out of the store to look for her, my face flushed with worry, I was stopped by a security guard. "Is everything okay?" he asked. "Are you lost?"

"Yes, sir," I answered, explaining that I'd gone to the Foot Locker to look for some shoes and had lost track of my mother.

"Don't worry," he said. "This happens all the time. I'll help you find her."

That time, the guard's presence calmed my quickly pounding heart. But the difficult thing about being Black in America is never knowing how people whose job it is to provide assistance will respond. Will it be "How can I help you?" or "Your Black body in this space makes me uncomfortable. What right do you have to be here?"

Doughnut Crumbs and Crack Rocks

My first encounter with real police officers took place during my junior year of high school. I owned a cream-colored Delta 88 that I'd bought and paid for myself. If you caught it at the right time of day, it might have passed for one of the Cutlasses or Cadillacs made famous by Outkast's music videos. Most girls were too savvy to confuse my car for anything worth their attention. For that reason, I preferred to drive my mother's white Mitsubishi Galant.

One Saturday night, my mother had gone to a basketball game at the high school. She was heavily involved in the PTA, so she was just as likely to go to these sporting events as I was. She'd taken the Delta 88 and left the Galant with me because I had a date. But before I could head out for the night, my mother called and let me know that she'd decided to come home, only the car wouldn't start.

Aware that things could quickly get out of hand after sporting events, especially when Johnson was playing a rival school, I jumped into her car and didn't think to follow the rules. The song "Notorious Thugs" was hot on the radio at the time. It featured a recently deceased Biggie Smalls and Bone Thugs-N-Harmony, with the kind of relentless drumbeat conducive to speeding, and it boomed from my speakers as I accelerated toward the school. I knew I was in trouble when I saw those flashing lights. After turning down my radio and pulling to the side of the road, I placed my hands on the steering wheel and waited.

I watched the officer approach in the rearview mirror; he looked as leery of me as I was of him.

"Where are you heading in such a hurry this time of night?" he said.

"I'm sorry, sir," I replied. "My mother's car broke down over at Johnson High School. I was worried and so I was rushing to get there."

My explanation and mention of my mother did not soften his glower. "That is no excuse for going fifty in a thirty-five. I am going to have to give you a ticket."

I took a deep breath. My mother would be upset, but she would understand my haste. All would be well.

Then the officer noticed something in the car. "What is that in the seat next to you? Is that cocaine?"

The accusation sent a chill through me. A speeding stop was one thing, but if this cop thought I was a drug dealer, there was no telling what he might do. I glanced over to my right, wondering if someone I'd given a ride to could have left something in the seat. But I didn't see anything. I stilled my fraying nerves and replied, "Sir, there is nothing in the seat that I can see."

Backing away, he yelled, "Get out of the car!"

I took my hands off the steering wheel, opened the door from the outside to keep them visible, and exited the car.

Within seconds, he'd handcuffed me and led me over to his police cruiser. He had not read me my rights, so I thought there was still a chance to de-escalate. "Sir," I asked, "would you please tell me what I have done wrong? I am not a drug dealer, and there are no drugs in my car." But he was in no mood to negotiate. When backup police cars arrived, I explained repeatedly from the back seat that I was just trying to get to my mom, but they informed me that I wasn't going anywhere until the drug specialist arrived to test the substance.

Meanwhile, the whole neighborhood drove past, gawking at the "good kid" who was supposedly on his way to college sitting there handcuffed like a common criminal.

It didn't make sense. I had followed my mother's rules all my life. Now fears and doomsday scenarios bounced off one another. *Had the officer planted something? Could I do time for possession? Will this ruin my chances at a scholarship?*

After what felt like hours, the drug specialist arrived. The officer who had handcuffed me pointed to the passenger seat. The new officer opened the passenger door, bent over, and came back with a substance on his finger. Shockingly enough, he put it in his mouth. Then he muttered something to the arresting officer, who, in turn, came over to me.

"You are free to go," he said, clearly attempting to hide the frustration lurking in the forced neutrality of his tone.

Shocked, I asked, "What about the ticket?"

"Just go home, son," he said.

When I got back in my car, I finally figured out what had caught his attention. A few days before, I had eaten some Krispy Kreme doughnuts in the car. Some of the flakes of icing had spilled and collected in the crevices of the passenger seat.

My mother was there when I got home, having found someone to jump-start the Delta 88. I recounted what had just happened. Having had a little time to process it, I found the police officers' embarrassment hilarious. (What can you do with the absurdity of anti-Black racism except to periodically laugh at it to avoid losing your mind?) When I concluded the story with "And this fool thought that doughnut crumbs was crack!," I expected a chuckle, but my mother did not give me one. Instead she said, "Haven't I told you how you are supposed to conduct yourself? You could have thrown your whole life away in a moment!"

My mom's fear unveiled a central reality of Black parenting: nothing is stable. I knew she wasn't screaming at me that night. She was yelling at a country that filled her with anxiety for her offspring. We could follow all the rules, but I might do something foolish, just like any teenager, and she knew that the cost of Black immaturity could be a shipwrecked life.

I have often wondered if that police stop was an incident of racism or incompetence, or a combination of the two. I believe the officer saw those sugary flakes as drugs because he expected to find illegal substances in a car driven by a young Black man listening to hip-hop. I'm sure white lawyers and doctors driving expensive cars in nice neighborhoods have been pulled over with Krispy Kreme fragments in their cars. I doubt they wound up handcuffed on the side of the road.

We can write laws that reform how police officers interact with the public. Legislation is important. But those laws are enforced by individuals. It is not just the laws that must be reformed but also the habitual suspicion of Black bodies. That suspicion is a matter of societal custom that goes beyond law enforcement, a sickness both legal and spiritual.

Parked While Black

About a year after the doughnut incident, I was with my girlfriend, talking in my car outside a friend's house, when a police car pulled up.

"What are you doing?" the officer asked.

I answered, "Talking to my girlfriend, Officer."

He asked for my license. I handed it to him, and he returned to the patrol car to key in my information. Upon his return, he had a much sterner look, and he ordered me out of the car and handcuffed me.

I asked the officer, "Excuse sir, what did I do? Why am I being arrested?"

He replied: "There is a warrant out for your arrest in connection to an armed robbery."

The accusation infuriated me. I had never robbed anyone, not even close, but Black men under investigation by the police are not afforded the luxury of displaying emotion. So I replied with the same tone that I might have used if the subject matter were littering rather than a felony. In the hopes of finding a way to clear my name, I asked, "When did this robbery occur?"

He answered, "In 1989."

I replied, "I was ten years old in 1989. You are looking for my father. He has the same name as I do."

The officer paused for a moment. "According to my records, his last known address is Ryland Pike. Is he still there?"

I answered, "I don't know. If you see him, tell him that he owes back child support," my deference slipping in a moment of frustration. I was seventeen years old with a beard and a football player's build, but there was no chance I could have been mistaken for a thirty-six-year-old man.

Getting Gas While Black

One Friday night, Brandon, Corey, and I all crowded into my Delta 88 and headed down University Drive, a central thruway in my hometown. I decided to stop and get some gas so that I wouldn't have to do so later, on the way home from a night of partying. Pulling into the gas station, we saw some of our friends from school and began to chat about our plans for the evening. They told us about a house party and suggested that we head there instead of the club, which sounded like a good idea to us.

As I pumped the gas, I noticed that an all-black SUV had pulled up right behind my car, and I thought, *That dude needs to fall back. I'll be done in a minute.* Then another SUV came in on the left and another on the right. By the time I got back into the car, we were surrounded.

Next, police officers came pouring out of those SUVs and rushed my car with flashlights. I thought, *Well, that is good news: flashlights, not guns.* They shouted, "Keep your hands where we can see them. Do not move! Get out of the car." I thought, *How do my friends not move and get out of the car?*

Slowly we exited.

Accustomed to the drill, I asked the cop closest to me, "What did we do, Officer?"

He replied, "This is a well-known drug hangout, and we saw you making a sale here a few moments ago."

This was also a well-known place to get gas on a Friday night, and that thought brought an unbidden smile to my face.

"Something funny?" the officer said.

"No, sir." I spoke slowly, trying to de-escalate the tension. "That was not a drug deal. Those were friends of ours inviting us to a party. Nothing more."

"Well," he told me, "I am going to need you all to sit over there by the store while we search your car." So we dutifully walked over. One officer stood guard while my car was searched from top to bottom, including the trunk.

I was furious, but what could I do? After they did not find anything, I asked the officer for his badge number: I had seen that on TV. He covered his badge.

They got in their SUVs, and they drove away while we sat silently for a few moments, too stunned by their actions to move.

Brandon was the one to break the silence: "Are you ready to go to the party?"

I replied that I was done for the night.

Time to Leave

A final encounter that took place when I was in college convinced me that I had to leave the South if I wanted to make it to my twenty-second birthday. Devin and I had come to Huntsville for the weekend to meet with members from the local chapters of Alpha Phi Alpha, Omega Psi Phi, and Kappa Alpha Psi at Alabama A&M. Having tried the white fraternities on campus and found them nonviable, we wanted to convince one of the Black fraternities to start a chapter at Sewanee. The meetings were even less successful than our experiments with white fraternities. Most of the conversations were brief and polite.

"What is the name of the school?"

"Sewanee."

"Like the river from the Ray Charles song?"

"No, that is the *Suwannee,* in Georgia. We are in Tennessee."

"How many potential members do you have?"

"We have about twenty Black males on campus, and most of them are interested."

The number twenty was a sticking point. They said, "We don't think that y'all can sustain a chapter on that campus. We just don't think it will work." Our mission to import a little Black culture into Sewanee had failed.

That Sunday evening, the two of us began the trip that would take us northeast, about a seventy-minute drive to campus. When southern Black folks travel, the question is not the best way to get from one city to another. We discuss the *safest* route. Alabama, Georgia, Louisiana, Mississippi, and Tennessee still have cities, towns, and neighborhoods that are no-go zones for Black people, a half century after the Civil Rights Movement. We keep an informal mental map of these towns. My mom always made me promise that under no circumstances would I ever to go to Cullman, Arab, or Good Springs, Alabama. I didn't even know where those places were. There was nothing to draw me there, but she made me give her my word.

Once, on my way back from Mississippi, I got off at a random exit because I needed gas. I walked into a station that also had a hamburger spot attached to it. When I stepped inside, I noticed that everyone was white and that no one seemed enthusiastic to see me. Black people know the meaning of that look and the best way to survive when we have stumbled into places bubbling with danger. I made a quick decision. Rather than fill up, I said to the attendant, "Can I have fifteen dollars regular on number four, please?" I handed him a twenty and said, "Keep the change." Fifteen dollars would give me enough fuel to take me to a major town and a safer exit. I returned to my car calmly but quickly and began pumping the gas. As I was finishing, a few people came out of the gas station and got in their pickups. They turned on their engines but did not move until I did. As I pulled out, they followed close behind and tailed my car until I returned to the highway.

Devin and I left Huntsville late because we'd stayed to watch a football game on television. Knowing that the route from Huntsville to Sewanee was dotted with small, predominantly white communities, my mom had suggested we stay the night with her, but we'd decided to head back to campus.

Making our way to Highway 64, we were driving along one of those patches of road marked by nothing more than the occasional gas station or dive bar when we passed a police car. I looked in my rearview mirror and saw the officer pull onto the road. I checked the speedometer and confirmed that I was not speeding.

"Do you see that?" I said to Devin.

"Yeah, I saw him."

"What do you think we should do?"

"Not much we can do at this point."

After being trailed for a few miles, we approached a town that was a known speed trap. Just past what in the dark looked like an auto repair shop, the speed limit dropped from fifty to thirty-five. Knowing that many college students had been caught unawares on their journey to campus, I made sure to be at thirty miles per hour when we reached that town. That was when the lights came on.

"I saw you made a sudden change of speed," the officer said after he pulled me over.

I explained that the speed limit had changed, but this did not satisfy him. "Where you *boys* heading?" he asked. Devin and I were both over twenty-one at the time.

I responded, "We are college students at Sewanee. We are going back to campus. We have classes tomorrow."

"I don't believe you," he said. "I need both of your licenses and your school IDs." He took our cards and went back to his car. After a few minutes, he returned with a warning: "You *boys* go straight to campus and do not stop any-where between here and there. You understand?"

Everything within me wanted to accept the invitation to resist his disrespect. I did not. But I did not know how many more times I could remain calm in the face of such blatant hostility. I had only so many more "yes, sir"s in me.

Most Black people can tell stories like these. If they don't, it's because encounters with the police are ordinary enough to hardly warrant their telling. Outsized acts of evil attract news cameras, but it is commonplace racism that makes us weary. I would go months without an incident, and then anti-Black sentiment would come knocking at my door, disrupting whatever peace I'd managed to find. Racism always demands our full attention and never follows a schedule.

I do not hate the police. I remember my mother dialing 911 on my father when I was a child. Officers would arrive at our house with empathy and concern for an endangered woman and her young children. But as I aged, I saw that empathy disappear.

My uncle Reggie was a cop for eight years. He helped start the Association of Black Police Officers in my home-town. Growing up, I heard stories of police officers encountering humanity at its most broken. He spoke about seeing people so strung out that they barely knew their names, about answering domestic-abuse calls in neighborhoods both white and Black. But he also saw his fellow officers say and do such racist things that he eventually left the force altogether.

I understand how witnessing the violence people inflict on each other could turn the most optimistic person into a cynic. I sympathize, but such sympathy does not dislodge the memory of my own dehumanizing encounters. If repeated exposure to humanity at its most broken does something to the souls of officers, I worried, what might repeated exposure to negative incidents with police officers do to mine? My frustrations sent me running from the South, hoping to find the warmth of other suns.

CHAPTER 8

There Is Power in the Blood

I still remember the night in 1987 when my mom gathered us around the TV to hear Ronald Reagan talk about the HIV crisis. In a somber tone, the president described a disease that could infect the blood through transfusions, drug use, or sex.

Blood. Drug use. Sex. As a child of eight, I was scared. I had relatives addicted to drugs; I had seen the needle in my father's arm when I'd stepped into the bathroom and discovered him shooting up. I could identify the mist in the eyes of people caught up in their latest high. Could my father, my uncles, or the addicts who wandered our neighborhood have AIDS? And what about me? How many playground scuffles had I been part of, returning home with scrapes on my knees and arms? I had surely exchanged blood with friends and foes.

Most childhood fears are simply matters of overidentification. Children see things on television and believe that what is recounted on the screen will happen to them. But AIDS was a real-life monster that came out into the world to hunt. Some experts reported the life expectancy for a patient to be two years from diagnosis to death. I hoped that our family would be spared.

At the time, we were at our poorest and living on my mother's disability checks, but she still had it in her heart to help others—especially our classmates and other women. Kids in my school took to calling her "Mother," because she kept tabs on them as if they were her own:

You staying in those books, Andre?

Jason, how is your sister? I hear that she has not been in school for a few days.

I heard you got kicked out of class for talking back to Mrs. Carter. I know your parents taught you better than that.

At church or school, if word had spread that a particular woman was having a rough time with her kids or her partner, my mother would pull her aside and talk to her. She even invited people to stay with us in our home, sharing our meager resources while they figured out their next steps. Her generosity arose in part from her school board connections; generous was also just what she was. John Wesley, the famous founder of Methodism, called the world his parish; my mother's parish was the world of Northwest Huntsville.

My cousin Clarice was among the women my mother sought to protect. She was a little older than me, with brown eyes and skin dark enough to prevent her from being considered mixed but lighter than my chocolate complexion. She had what they called "baby hair," fine locks with natural, loose curls. Her smile suggested a world of mirth that she shared with her closest friends. I grew up hearing my mom, aunties, and uncles say that Clarice would drive boys crazy when she got older, though I didn't understand what that meant. I only knew that I found her beautiful. By the time I was eight, I could see that this opinion was shared by boys her age, along with older men. But like so many life-defining events, the interactions between her and the teen boy from whom she would contract HIV were beside the point. They dated for a while, had sex, and she got pregnant, neither of them knowing that anything was amiss. Although her first child died shortly after birth, she wouldn't be diagnosed with AIDS until the death of her *second* child.

AIDS was stigmatizing. But to me, Clarice was still the cool cousin I looked up to. It was impossible for me to process the idea that someone who looked normal and healthy was sick and could be dying. In this, I was not alone. Many of our family members could not accept that she had AIDS:

Clarice don't got no AIDS, it's cancer.

Where could she get some AIDS from?

It's just a rare blood disease. That side of the family always coming down with something.

It wasn't just aunts and uncles who seemed not to understand the reality of Clarice's illness. Clarice seemed blind to it as well. Two of her children died before she was diagnosed, and she had three more children afterward who survived because they received antiviral treatments that prevented the disease from being passed to them. Still, so little was known and understood in those days. According to my mother, Clarice told some of the men she dated that she had AIDS, but they did not seem to be afraid.

When Clarice became truly ill, fear replaced my family's denial. Friends and relatives stopped inviting her over for meals. Those who did gave her disposable plates and cups to eat and drink from. During post-dinner conversation, some stopped sitting next to her on the couch. Clarice tried to defy their judgments at first, laughing and talking and eating at their houses regularly as though nothing had changed.

When Clarice got so ill that she could not take care of herself, my mom sat us down and explained to us that our cousin would be staying in our home. She said that it would be just like when Grandma Laura had once invited us into hers.

But it was nothing like our time at Grandma Laura and Granddad Theodore's. Clarice arrived at our house in pain, with lesions on her face and body. Doctors had given her an ointment to relieve the discomfort, but she was often too weak to apply it. The experimental drug regimens caused her energy and her pain levels to fluctuate wildly. A change in dosage could take her from looking close to death to recovery. We never knew which Clarice we were going to encounter, but we saw her many times each day because she slept where every guest did, on the living room couch next to the dining room table, where her presence was unavoidable. Some days she had energy; others she just lay there. When Clarice was unable to apply the pain-relieving ointment herself, my mother would rub it into her arms, legs, back, and thighs. The visible signs of her illness scared me, and I am ashamed to say that I did not want to be near her.

My memory of Clarice at that time crystalizes around one particular day. Coming home hungry after another long day of middle school, I'd placed a freshly cooked batch of French fries in our white mixing bowl and drenched them with ketchup. Being that there was no other place to watch television, I took my snack to the living room. That afternoon Clarice was having a good day, more alert than usual. Rising from the couch she had claimed as her own, she came over and sat beside me on the love seat. "Can I have some fries?" she asked when she saw what I was eating. "I'm starving."

I looked up at her and studied the lesions on her skin, as well as the bruises and the split lip one of her boyfriends had given her. The wound was a few weeks old, but I wondered if blood could still seep out of it. There would have been no way to tell if she bled into the ketchup-soaked French fries.

At church, we had listened to sermons about blood. A favorite of our pastor's focused on the evening before God liberated the Israelites from bondage to the Egyptians. That night, God gave them instructions: *Wipe the blood of the lamb over the doorposts of your home, because the angel of death is about to pass through Egypt.* Any home marked with this blood would be passed over by the angel. The preacher promised us that if we surrendered our lives to Christ, we would be marked by the blood of the lamb, and death would have no power over us. Barely a Sunday went by without him preaching about it. We had a thousand different songs about the blood of the lamb, but there was one that always got the older members of the congregation going. The chorus went, "There is power, power, wonder-working power, in the blood of the lamb."

I feared the sickness that could be contained in a single drop of blood, but I also knew that people had started to avoid Clarice, and I could imagine how lonely she must have felt. And I knew, too, that even though her beauty had been ravaged by AIDS, she was the same Clarice I had loved my whole life. After saying a silent prayer that the power of the blood of Jesus might overrule that of the virus, I extended my arm with the bowl of fries. "Yes. Sure, cousin."

Clarice smiled and reached her hand into the bowl. Our fingers touched, and we ate. It was a communion of sorts, a sharing of sadness, longing, and hope.

When Clarice moved into our house, I thought that she would die there. She did not. With adjustments to her medications, her health improved, and she was able to move out of our home. Clarice was always an independent spirit, and she wanted to live on her own. Her return to independence was possible due to a financial settlement she received from Huntsville Hospital.

Clarice's involvement with the hospital had begun about a decade earlier, when she gave birth to her firstborn, Henry, when she was only fifteen. Two weeks later, Henry fell ill. Clarice took him to the local urgent care center, where a doctor, noting his elevated fever, inconsolable crying, and strange grunting noises, told Clarice that Henry needed to be taken to the emergency room. She went straight to Huntsville Hospital but was sent away because she had neither insurance nor the $54 fee. They instructed her to give Henry a bath and some Tylenol.

My grandmother Laura remembers Clarice rushing into her home frantic and cussing up a storm. "My baby is sick and these folks won't f*cking help him! He won't stop crying. And they won't do a d*mn thing. I don't know what to do!"

Grandma Laura lent her the $54, and Clarice rushed back to the hospital with Henry. It was eight P.M. by the time she made it there, and in the interim his condition had worsened. It would take another three hours for him to be seen. He would breathe his last breath the next afternoon. The timeline is painful to recount because so many precious hours were wasted. Clarice spent the last hours of Henry's life pleading with the staff for him to be treated. The doctors diagnosed the cause of death as spinal meningitis. We know now that the ultimate cause was the fact that he had been born with AIDS.

Refusing to accept the casting aside of her baby, Clarice sued the hospital. When the lower court ruled against her, she appealed. The case made it all the way to the Alabama Supreme Court, which ruled in her favor. Her victory set a precedent that opened the path for others to sue Huntsville Hospital for negligence.

I never met Henry. His death and the long fight for justice occurred when I was still learning my ABC's. I didn't know anything about the court battle while it was happening, but by the time Clarice moved in with us, I had learned what had befallen her baby, and I considered her courageous for taking on an entire hospital system and a deadly disease at the same time. In doing so, Clarice taught me something about humanity: it doesn't matter if your chances of victory are slim to nonexistent; you have to demand respect, even from a largely indifferent system.

A few years after she'd lived with us, her health started to fail again. Our last meeting took place in a hospital during my sophomore year of high school. Dressed in the clumsy blue gowns and surgical masks that would become commonplace twenty-five years later, during the COVID-19 pandemic, we were told that her immune system had become so severely compromised that even a sneeze could transmit germs that would kill her.

Clarice had been drifting in and out of sleep over the last few days, and she would not awaken when we visited. I stared at her and watched her chest slowly rise and fall. I hoped that some profound final goodbye would come to me when I needed it most, some speech that might communicate to her how much she meant to me as a kid. But I had no words, no wisdom or declaration to make. I sat silently beside her, the way I'd done at our house so many years ago, and then I left. She died peacefully later that week.

I do not recall her memorial service, but I do remember the viewing that took place in the funeral home the day before. She looked like my cousin again, as beautiful in death as she had been in life. She appeared to be at peace, finally at rest from her labors.

She left behind gifts for her family. A while before she'd passed, Clarice had taken out life insurance so that her children would have resources with which to build their lives after she was gone. According to the insurer's terms, she had to live at least two years before the policy would fully vest.

When my mom was cleaning out the last home Clarice lived in, she found her journals. In them Clarice recounted the doctor's visits when she would receive updates about her T-cell count. She wrote that she would sit in the doctor's office preaching to those T-cells: "I told them T-cells to be fruitful and multiply like the five loaves and two fish Jesus made into a feast." Those T-cells listened long enough for the policy to take effect. Clarice made it the full two years and died a few weeks after the policy vested. She fought until the end for the sake of her children. After she died, they were adopted by our relatives. Other mothers took up her work and raised them as their own.

Clarice left one more unexpected gift for my mother and our family. She used the money she won in her lawsuit against Huntsville Hospital to buy a tiny home on Mount Vernon Road, off Blue Spring Road. The house was smaller and more run-down than our 1,250-foot Sandia residence, but it was hers, the vine and fig tree revisited. She lived with her children in that home for a few years, but she would not get the chance to see them reach maturity. After she died, the house went into foreclosure. My grandfather Theodore would pay the fees to keep it in the family. Around a year or so later, when my own family hit financial rock bottom and my mother couldn't afford to pay rent, we moved into that house on Mount Vernon. We lived there during my junior and senior years of high school. Clarice's courage gave us a place to stay.

When death comes for us, we have decisions to make.

We can run from the fear that proximity to death produces in us, or we can love. My cousin lived with a disease that few of us understood, even those closest to her. But she fought despite those odds. She fought just like Sophia and Wavon for a place to call her own. That her victories were somewhat fleeting doesn't make them any less glorious.

Part III

═══

ORDINARY GLORY

CHAPTER 9

If You Scared Go to Church

My sophomore year of high school, I met a girl at a party. I wanted to see her again, but this was before electronic devices took over, which meant she gave me her number and we talked on the phone for a few weeks before finally setting a date. She lived in the Lincoln Park projects, a few miles south of my neighborhood near downtown Huntsville, an area I knew only vaguely. Lacking the advantages of GPS, I relied on her directions when I drove down to pick her up, but I couldn't find her house. Before giving up, I decided to get out and walk, thinking it might be easier for her to spot me.

That was a mistake. While I'd been driving around searching for her address, the locals must have noticed my car circling their block. A group of young men came over.

One of them asked, "Who are you?" His tone invited confrontation: *You have stepped into my territory. Why are you here?*

Looking around at the plastic bags blowing in the wind, clothes drying on flimsy lines, weeds fighting a losing battle amid patches of dirt that might have been a yard, I could not see anything worth fighting over. But behind the interrogator stood three or four more young men, one with a gun. The weapon changed the stakes of the conversation: it was no longer an inquiry about my reasons for being in the neighborhood but a question of life and death.

A rush of adrenaline began in my chest. I could not control my rapid heart rate. The only thing I could control was my expression, so I adopted a calm exterior.

Experience had taught me to recognize the difference between killers and posers. A certain coldness of the eye resides in the stares of the truly violent; the rest of us fake what comes naturally to the genuinely cruel. These boys looked like me and my friends, caught up in a role-playing ritual. Still, having been in this situation before, I knew that I would have to navigate it in such a way that they didn't feel trapped. I had to be strong but not threatening, certain but not disrespectful.

Who are you? The situation called for a simple statement of my allegiances: *I am from Johnson High, and where I live is not your concern.* But maybe because there was a gun involved, the question of who I was turned existential. I thought, *Who am I, really?* A boy grown into his adult body, now capable of wielding the same violence I'd witnessed from my father? A kid determined to be the opposite of that man? My mother's hope? At sixteen, I was a mix of competing visions and possibilities, with nothing to tie them together.

What came next surprised even me. "I am a Christian," I responded.

If breath and sound could be chased down, I would have run after my words and dragged them back inside my mouth. But it was too late. I had spoken.

The boys were shocked. I could see it on their faces. Of all the responses and explanations, that was not one they'd expected. They'd wanted me to say that I wasn't from there, so that they could be justified in resorting to violence. But to hear that they were in the presence of a church kid must have thrown them off-balance. In response, they laughed and walked away.

We used to say, *If you scared, go to church,* meaning that faith was for the weak and the cowardly who found street life too much for them. But it wasn't fear of a violent outcome that had motivated my confession. I'd had a moment of God-given clarity.

We do not know who we are until we are forced to decide under the pressure of life-and-death situations. These moments, as much as any statement of belief, reveal the role that God plays in our lives. Sophia heard God the clearest with a gun in her hands; my mom heard God in a hospital room on the way to surgery; my cousin Clarice turned to God when her T-cell counts went low. I did not hear the voice of God in that moment. It was more like God erupted out of me, from some hidden place that I didn't know existed. For good or ill, I knew that day that my life was in some sense bound up with my Creator.

．　．　．

I returned home from the stalled confrontation and told no one what I'd said. Two years would pass before I had the courage to take the step that part of me must have sensed was coming. I would go to church and tell the pastor that I felt called to preach. It was the same step my grandfather Theodore had taken decades before when he'd entered the ministry.

My maternal grandfather looms large in my childhood imagination. Theodore Bone was born in 1937 in Gurley, Alabama, not far from where Sophia, my father's grandmother, purchased her plot of land. Like Sophia, my grandfather picked cotton alongside the rest of his family, beginning at age five. Unlike Sophia, he managed to get some schooling. He attributes his love of learning to his paternal grandfather, Willie H. Bone. Willie and his wife, Fannie, raised him when their teenage daughter Clara found having a child too much to handle. Like me, he would always struggle with the feeling of abandonment.

My grandfather's future success as a businessman and community leader shows that he had a good mind, even if the segregated schools of rural Alabama rarely gave him room to show it. The Black kids working the fields outnumbered those in the classrooms, and schools often shut down so that children could help their parents work land they did not own. Only on limited occasions was effort taken to stretch Black minds.

Against a backdrop of oppression, self-reflection and long-term planning were viewed as minor rebellions. Grandfather remembers his early years of resistance well. He took his own grandfather's advice to heart and embraced education as a means of escaping the fields. "I didn't want to pick cotton my whole life," he told me. "I wanted to learn."

Excited to go to school every day, he dressed and fed himself, then waited for the school bus to pick him up while his grandparents saw to their morning chores. He remembers the mud flaps on the side of the bus and the driver, Mr. Freeman, who drove all the "colored children" to their segregated three-room school. Along the way, they passed buildings limited to white people, all much nicer than theirs. When they arrived at their own shanty, the children had to start a fire to warm the place. My grandfather used to joke that by the time the place got good and warm, school was ending. He recalls being either cold in the classroom or hot in the fields, but never particularly comfortable, his Black body never fully at rest.

Theodore's family farmed fifteen acres of land owned by a white man named Rude Miller. The profits were split forty-sixty. My family's 40 percent paid for all the necessities that made the land productive: seed, fertilizer, agricultural equipment, labor, mules, and horses. Week in and week out, Rude Miller took the profit from their labor and their risk, and at the end of the year he would tell them, "You almost made it." Rather than a paycheck, my grandfather received a pair of shoes, some overalls, three meals a day, and some used books. But disrespecting a white man in the 1930s and 1940s could lead to a lynching, so the terms were nonnegotiable.

My grandfather's life speaks to the disadvantages of institutionalized and structural racism in twentieth-century

America—racism that permeated everything from the farm to the classroom to the grocery store. My grandfather missed significant school time because his family needed him to pick cotton if they wanted to break even or have the hope of realizing a profit. In turn, Miller's family reaped wealth they did not deserve.

Every moment my grandfather spent under the white gaze was one in which he was forced to know his place; and that place was closed in on every side. But Willie H. Bone, Theodore's grandfather, refused to accept the arrangement. Nobody knows exactly how he did it, but he managed to put aside a dollar here and quarter there over the years. Then, like Moses descending from Sinai, he showed up at the courthouse in Huntsville one day with $1,500 and purchased a home. Returning to the farm, he collected his wife and family. As my grandfather remembers it, Willie told Rude, "We don't work here no more."

Starting then, my grandfather lived with ten members of his family in a three-bedroom house on Hall Street, located within a pleasant three- or four-block stretch that was known for being a respectable Black neighborhood. To fund their new life, Willie found a job digging ditches for the city. My grandfather remembers, "There was a colored school right across the street. It still wasn't as nice as the white school across town, but it was ours. I could walk there. I think my father moved us there hoping that would give me a chance to make up some ground academically."

Brown v. Board of Education would integrate the schools across America in 1954, the year my grandfather completed eighth grade, at age sixteen. A United Press International image of Nettie Hunt seated atop the steps of the Supreme Court, newspaper in hand, announced the significance of integration for the collective imagination: the world had changed. But change rarely occurs as it is remembered. Huntsville would not follow through with integration for another nine years, making the aftermath of *Brown* more like the period between Emancipation and Juneteenth. My grandfather does not remember *Brown* as a seminal event. His home had no television, no newspaper. That verdict passed without any discussion in his neighborhood. He never attended an integrated school. His oldest daughter, Vanessa, would not do so until the third grade.

Having missed countless classroom hours to work in the fields, Theodore concluded his ninth-grade year at the age of seventeen. Already a man, hardened by years of intense labor in the scorching Alabama sun, he left school and took a job at the RC Cola factory, mixing large vats of grape and orange soda from five A.M. to six P.M. for $17 per week. When one of his teachers saw that he wasn't in school, he reached out. My grandfather recalls telling him, "I ain't got no clothes to wear to school or food to eat." The teacher suggested that he join the military and finish his education there.

That plan seemed as good as any, so he joined the U.S. Army in 1956 and served for three years, stationed in Greenland and Labrador. While in the military, he finished his schooling and took classes on bookkeeping and finances. By the time I was born, he had parlayed those skills into his own business, T & L Records, a music store that stocked blues,

R&B, gospel, and hip-hop. Most of the sales were cassettes and CDs, but you could still get actual vinyl records. He also pastored St. James Presbyterian Church in Decatur.

Between the two incomes, he made a pretty good living. He owned the home where my family gathered for every major holiday—the biggest and nicest dwelling of any member of the family. He was, in many ways, the picture of Black success. Black people greeted him in the grocery stores and avoided making eye contact with him when exiting liquor stores. He was one of the few men in my family who did not abandon his wife and children.

One story he liked to recount was his conversion and call. No pastor worth his weight in salt enters the ministry without a call, an inner compulsion or feeling that God is commanding you to serve his people. In the Black tradition, the "call" describes a desire to preach the Gospel, which is different from an experience of God's love. All Christians have that. The call is a sense of being commissioned to a task that requires more than one feels capable of giving. Who, after all, would take it upon themselves to speak about the things of God? Most clergy talk about trying to run from it, but the hound of heaven won't leave them be until they relent.

My grandfather remembers being drawn to the faith at an early age: "My grandparents who raised me were religious, but my grandmother got too frail to go to church. Something in me wanted to learn about God. So I started walking to church by myself at the age of twelve. It was a couple of miles, but I had friends who would go with me."

The summer when he was sixteen, a nearby chapel

hosted a revival service. In those days, revivals went on every day for three weeks. The first two weeks consisted of prayer services; the last week, preaching. By the time the preaching started, people were primed and ready to shout and praise the Lord. Listening to the guest preacher proclaim the power of Jesus's blood, my grandfather felt God pulling at him: "I resisted as long as I could. But after about the third day of preaching, I gave my life to Christ. I felt the call toward the ministry even then, but I tried to serve God in other ways."

Pastors were not always held in high esteem, and there is both joy and resignation in my grandfather's voice when he recalls how he received his calling. "Lots of people assumed that preachers were in it just for the money," he told me. "The clergy were called 'chicken eaters' because most of the time preachers were paid in food instead of cash. Most often chickens. One preacher did such a good job that they gave him a coop's worth of chickens after preaching a revival!" Pastors were seen as too lazy to get a real job that paid more, content to eke out a living one chicken at a time. My grandfather didn't want to be seen as just another pastor preaching for food. He was a genuine leader with convictions, not a charlatan preying on the insecurities of unsuspecting congregants.

For a long time that call built up within Theodore's five-foot-seven frame. He tried to quell it by singing in gospel quartets, traveling dusty roads with his fellow musicians, performing in churches and bars while sleeping in segregated spaces all across the South. The last band he formed, the Sons of Glory, even put out an album in the 1960s—

tossed aside, I'm sure, in the attic of some aging Black church member somewhere between Arkansas and Mississippi. I hope to find that recording one day.

The Sons of Glory had been on the road for a few weeks, trying to drum up support for their recently released album. One particular night found Theodore and his group in Tullahoma, Tennessee, singing in front of a packed church. He'd started in on one of his favorite songs, "Leave You in the Hands of the Lord," when the call came: "It felt like I was floating up in the air, but the next thing I knew, I wasn't in the sky, but lying on the ground. I don't recall how I got there. It couldn't have been too long, maybe thirty seconds or so, but I got up and finished the song. Then I told my bandmates, 'I can't wait no longer. I have to go and preach.'"

His first revival took place in Knoxville, Tennessee, more than two hundred miles from Huntsville. He gave everything he had in the five days he preached there, sweating through his suit and exhorting the little congregation to be washed in the blood of Jesus and have their sins wiped away. At the end of the week, he did not walk away with any chickens. He received, instead, a foot-long hot dog and fries. "But I kept preaching anywhere they would have me," he says, laughing.

Eventually he would get his own church, where my mother and her sisters would watch him work himself into a frenzy, declaring the glories of the Lord Sunday after Sunday.

My grandfather met my grandmother in a church—where else?—before he joined the ministry. The way he tells it, she sang in the choir and he was drawn in by her voice.

But when he told her he'd experienced a call to preach, she replied, "The Lord didn't call *me*."

My grandmother's beautiful singing voice made her a natural for the role of first lady, a title that Black churches bestow on the wife of the pastor. In his imagination, she would be Christian piety personified, leading the choir and making sure all the children were well behaved. But as my grandfather's pull toward God got stronger over the years, my grandmother resisted more firmly the role of first lady. She never raised her voice or lost her temper, but her fiercely independent spirit prevented her from being well suited to the job. So what if she spoke to one woman after the service and not another? Or if she sang what was thought to be too many solos in the choir? She did not want to be the source of pettiness among women who liked to gossip about favoritism or her children's too-casual dress.

A little while after she married my grandfather, she began playing bingo. The game was a chance to have fun away from the watchful eye of the congregation, and she started spending less time at church and more at the bingo hall. After bingo came cards and the lottery. What started as a pastime became an addiction, and soon she was taking trips down to Mississippi to gamble there.

The pastorate and its endless supply of chickens could not fund her habit the way gambling could. When a local numbers runner approached her about joining his network, she agreed. She'd compile bets and keep her tally on hand to verify the winners, and soon bettors were arriving at my grandparents' house with their lists of three- and four-number combinations. They bet their birthdays, anniversaries, phone numbers—any combination of numbers that meant something to them.

While betting centers could be found all over the city, gambling at the pastor's house felt safe and not so sinful. This made my grandparents' house the go-to spot. As a child, I'd watch the endless stream of poor Black people going in and out of my grandparents' home, hoping to strike it rich. More often than not, they failed. But I wished for their luck alongside them because they could be generous when they won. On a good day I'd find myself walking home with a ten- or even a twenty-dollar bill.

On weekends, my grandmother hosted card games downstairs while my grandfather sat in his office preparing the next day's sermon. My aunt Mary cooked up platters of fried chicken and fish, dutifully delivered to the players by us grandchildren. We would gather as a family on Friday and Saturday nights in the makeshift gambling hall of my grandparents' home. Then on Sunday we went together to the house of the Lord.

My grandparents pastored in different worlds: the speakeasy and the pulpit. This collision of vocations informed my understanding of Christianity. Many of the gamblers were church members, and several of the church members were gamblers, which is to say that the church was never separate from the world. The saints came to church along with the sinners. Both existed in the same congregation, in the same household, in the same person.

But not everyone appreciated that collision of cultures. As the years passed and the rumors began to mount, church members came to see the pastor's home as the center of scandal. The church leadership decided to intervene, citing the sale of rap music out of my grandfather's record shop as being contrary to Christian principles. It was time for my grandfather to go. After pastoring at St. James for twenty-seven years, my grandfather took a job at Beaver Dam Primitive Baptist Church, a smaller congregation outside the city where the congregants spoke with thick southern country accents. He would pastor there for twenty years before retiring completely from the ministry.

As a youth, I was upset that my grandfather didn't put a stop to the gambling. He never gambled himself, but having it in the house seemed like a tacit endorsement. When I envisioned my ministry, I wanted to be different. I didn't want to have a scandal that brought shame on the church. I didn't want to confirm people's worst opinions about Christianity.

It wasn't until it came time to prepare my father's eulogy that I worked up the courage to ask my grandfather the question that had plagued me all my life. I said, as respectfully as I could, "Granddad, why did you allow gambling to occur in your house? You had to know how it impacted the way people viewed you."

He hesitated before answering. I think he'd always known that one day he was going to have to explain this to the grandchild who'd followed him into the ministry. "I have always blamed myself for her addiction," he began. "I introduced her to bingo, and I was gone so much during the early years of our marriage, singing and preaching. I tried everything that I could to get her to stop, but she would not. What could I do? I couldn't leave her."

This rocked me. I had always blamed my father for leaving. Now I realized that I'd unknowingly blamed my grandfather for staying. His confession taught me about the complexity of adult decisions. His community had judged him harshly and wrongly for the better part of two decades, and he had borne that judgment for the sake of love. His worst nightmare had become true. Despite his best efforts, he had become known as a "chicken eater." But he wasn't. Things aren't so simple. He understood that love sometimes means acknowledging and bearing with the broken parts of people, even to the point of suffering scorn.

I was a child when my mother left her father's church and joined Union Hill Primitive Baptist, which was located at the intersection of multiple parts of Black Northwest Huntsville. Because it was within driving distance of the projects, the starter homes for working poor families, and the larger houses of the Black middle class, everyone came, the struggling alongside the comfortable; in this way it was not much different from my grandmother's Saturday nights, except that the communion wafer, not the poker table, took center stage. The entire spectrum of the Black community was there. Two-parent households with fathers in three-piece suits and mothers in fancy flower-filled hats sat next to the daring young girls who wore pants to church. All of them squeezed into the pews to listen to the music that had carried our people for centuries and to hear sermons that provided the counterargument to the nihilism that said things will always be the way they always have been.

Much of the music we sang in that church is not written

in any songbook that I've been able to locate. The only way to learn those songs was to attend service. An old deacon or mother of the church would make her way to the front and kneel just in front of the dais leading to the pulpit. With no accompaniment, her tired, weary voice would begin the spirituals composed on cotton fields by shackled Black bodies longing for freedom. When she went into another round of "I'm on My Way to Canaan Land" or "Swing Low, Sweet Chariot," the air would grow thick with the presence of God. Even the most hardened among us felt it.

Next came the choirs—clusters of caramel and chocolate bodies adorned in flowing green-and-white robes singing passionately and clapping in a rhythm my uncoordinated body could not match. Every now and then, shouts of praise for the goodness of the Lord would interrupt the singing when the Spirit would "fall."

As a kid, I saw that the Spirit could fall upon anybody—rich women in fancy dresses or poor folks in sweatpants, deacons in tailored suits or mothers of the church in their customary all-white uniforms. It was terrifying. Having been taught that control meant safety, I did not want the Holy Ghost to catch me if that would mean running up and down the aisles with little control over my body.

The pastor's sermon served as the climax of every service. But the pastor did not preach in monologues. The Black church adheres to the tradition of call and response, so that when Pastor Montgomery made a good point, he could expect a hearty *Amen* or *That's right* or *Come on now*. If his sermon wasn't going well, the congregation jumped in with a *Help him, Lord!*

Together, pastor and congregation struck a harmony that neither could replicate without the other, turning the church into a place of encounter, a meeting between the power of God and the temptation toward despair that comes from a life of poverty. So many of us dropped out, got involved with drugs, or just aimlessly drifted through life. These sermons willed us to believe for "just a little while longer now," as the deacons and mothers of the church used to say.

Wherever they began, the sermons all had the same destination. This was known as the "close," the climax in which the preacher invited everyone present to become a Christian or to renew their commitment to God. The key to an effective close was the slow building of tempo. Rather than turn to the cross straightaway, it was better to open with a question:

"I know a man that can help you. Can I tell you about him?"

Speak on him, Pastor. Speak on him.

"He came in human form after forty and two generations."

Yes, he did.

"He was born of a virgin in a stable with no place to lay his head. When he was born, the shepherd ran to see him, the angel choir lauded him, and the wise men sought him out."

Yes, they did!

"He was a wonder-worker. Demons feared him, sickness fled from those he touched, and even the winds and the seas obeyed him."

Amen! Yes, sir!

"There wasn't anyone like him before, and there ain't been nobody since. He is the King of Kings and Lord of Lords! But he was a man of constant sorrows, betrayed by those who should have loved him."

The close would exalt Jesus's earthly ministry and lament what happened next. But God was at work even in the bad news of Jesus's betrayal. God on the cross reconciled the world to himself. Had you gambled, drunk, lied, or cheated the night before? It didn't matter. Straying from the church didn't, either. There was always a chance to start anew. A lot of us "began again" week after week, caught in an endless cycle of sin and repentance. But the climax was the Resurrection, which signaled God's victory over our great enemy, death.

"The grave couldn't hold him!"

Say that, Pastor!

"The devil tried to stop him."

Amen!

"But *early* Sunday morning . . . he got up with all power!"

Yes he did, God.

It drove the congregation into a frenzy. The close made or broke a sermon; it was the difference between a fleeting moment and an experience of something that defied explanation.

Every Sunday was a battle between me and the Holy Spirit. I wanted to escape Sunday with my guard up and my sins comfortably in place. I wasn't a drug dealer, nor did I use, but that wasn't because of piety. I was simply terrified of what drugs would turn me into. Still, I could be cruel and biting, especially with my words. My conscience needled me for making fun of a kid who had the misfortune of being poorer and more haggardly attired than me. I'd made him cry because I was having a bad day. At home and at school, I cursed and lied. I lied so convincingly that I often began to believe my own stories. I lied to my mom when I stayed out too late, lied to my teachers to explain missing assignments, lied to my friends about girls I'd dated.

My older sister remembers one fabrication particularly well. Once, when we were jumping on my bed—something my mother had told us not to do—I bounced too high and fell off; my back hit the bed frame's railing, leaving a huge gash. Blood flowed everywhere. When my mom rushed in and asked what happened, I said, "Tasha pushed me." I didn't want to get in trouble.

My mom rushed me to the hospital, where I got sixteen stitches in my back. The scar is still visible. My sister vehemently denied pushing me, but she was punished and grounded for the better part of the summer, and I remained silent about my lie. This happened when we were kids, but I kept up the lie all through high school. Even when my sister revisited the accident and attempted to relitigate the case, I persisted. Although the lie no longer served a purpose, I stuck to it out of habit and, possibly, spite, clinging to my chance to mar the record of my too-perfect older sister.

I had a lot of sins to confess on Sundays. I didn't fight often, but when I did, I scrapped with abandon. And I hid it well, but I was angry all the time. With my father, with the people in my school and my neighborhood who seemed to confirm the worst stereotypes about Black America, with the addicts and dealers, with the cops and the Americans who normalized traumatizing Black people. I was angry, and I didn't want to change.

Giving my life fully to God was frightening, because I didn't know what God would do with me. I didn't want to practice the teachings of Christianity. Central to the Christian faith was the idea that we should love our enemies. At Johnson High, I had learned to crush them before they crushed me.

But that day in the Lincoln projects, when I found that I couldn't hate those boys who wanted to hurt me—for a brief moment, I saw them as God must see us all, trapped in habits and cycles that bring death and not life. Defending our neighborhood was all we knew how to do—even if no one else valued it, including the city that built and failed to maintain the projects and would order them to be torn down in the coming decades. Our little corner of the world was fading away, even as we fought to protect it.

I think those boys were so angry precisely because it was such a pitiful kingdom. The Lincoln projects were known as one of the roughest parts of the city. No one would call my neighborhood wealthy or even middle-class, but we lived in individual houses, not rows upon rows of the same decaying reddish-brown brick buildings. I knew that the people who lived there weren't so different from me, only a little more desperate.

If we were both trapped in the same tired play, then the

only way to change things was to rewrite the script. But who could tell a better story than the one we already knew? God was the answer that came to me that afternoon.

After church one Sunday, I asked Pastor Montgomery if I could meet with him during the coming week. My plan was to tell him that I'd been called to preach. It had taken years for that confession to make sense—all the way until graduation, when the question of my future forced me to be honest about my slowly forming plan.

When I walked into his office a few days later, I found him sitting at a large oak desk covered with books, papers, and an open King James Bible. He was apparently working on the next week's sermon. Hearing me approach, he glanced up and waited for me to speak, regarding me with a look of calm authority.

The words came tumbling out. I told him that I knew about the blood and forgiveness central to Christianity, but I also felt called to talk about what came after, the different path open for us with God as our pillar of fire, leading us through the desert. My ministry would be for people searching for hope among the rubble. My neighborhood had offered me a host of ways of ordering a human life—the potential methods for finding meaning, value, and purpose. In the end, only Christianity struck me as truly beautiful and transcendent. I aimed to appeal to young Black boys and girls considering the same options given to me, carrying traumas similar to the ones I had experienced. They had heard and rejected the church's offer. I wanted to ask them to reconsider their rejection.

When I told this to my pastor, he did not seem surprised, recalling how I came from a family of Black preachers. The McCaulleys and Bones tended toward binaries. We chose the church or the streets.

"If I were you, I would try and talk God out of it," he said with a laugh. "But I know that you won't. You have always been a determined kid. I've watched you struggle with purpose most of your life. I trust that you've finally found it. You haven't had it easy, McCaulley. I know that your family life is hard, but if you stick with God, he'll stick with you."

He explained that in three months, I would have to give a trial sermon. "Make sure that you mention the birth, death, Resurrection, and return of Jesus. Whatever else you get wrong, get Jesus right."

After muttering a few more sentences, I fled as if from a burning building, to prepare a sermon for the congregation.

Sophia had won. I had chosen the God of my ancestors. But the idea of preaching a sermon in front of a congregation of my friends and neighbors undid me. I knew what Black preaching was. All my life I had seen the staccato, structured, yet seemingly improvisational performance that involved both the preacher and the people. Every pastor I'd heard was a whooping preacher, which meant that they punctuated their sentences with a *huh* while rocking back and forth.

I knew all the words and gestures required of me, but I was not sure I could perform them. Try as I might, when I sat down to write, my ideas about God did not pour forth in sentences accentuated by pauses. Instead, paragraphs of uninterrupted reflections oozed out. I had things to say about God that needed to be said, and once I started, I didn't know how to find the pause. Much to my surprise, I was not good at writing Black sermons.

I concluded that the close, that crescendo of Black preaching, must itself be a work of the Spirit. Once I was in the pulpit, God would show up and teach me how to preach like my grandfather and my pastor. And so, a few months after receiving the call to preach, I ascended into the pulpit of Union Hill Primitive Baptist Church on a Sunday evening.

Because Sunday mornings can attract a thousand congregants, young preachers are often given the evening service, which draws a smaller crowd of a few hundred. I ascended the pulpit with a six-page sermon, a King James Bible, and a handkerchief, in case I worked up a sweat. But it turned out I was not that type of preacher. As my sermon wore on, I looked at the audience and saw them waiting for the shouted lines. Jaws dropped open to shout *Amen,* then closed again. People rose from their seats to clap, then thought better of it. The problem that plagued my sermon showed up in the preaching of it. I didn't have the pauses for the *Amen*s and *Yes, Lord*s. Despite my extensive preparation, I was still an eighteen-year-old kid trying to wrestle the idea of God into words, my sermon filled more with questions than applause lines. I could see that the congregation didn't know where they fit in the process or what to do with me. I asked myself, *Is this what God requires of me, this slow death in front of friends and family?*

Before I preached that first sermon, I had already been scheduled to deliver my second. My grandfather, after hearing of my call, had invited me into his pulpit across town. Again, most of that sermon is lost, just a hazy memory. I do remember that my grandfather apologized to the congregants after I'd finished: *He is just getting started. He will get better.* The Holy Spirit had apparently failed to show up again.

I carried on. My grand embarrassment occurred on New Year's Eve. In the Black church we have a service called "Watch Night." It recalls December 31, 1862, when the enslaved waited for the Emancipation Proclamation to go into effect on New Year's Day 1863. They passed the time praising God, singing, and preaching. That tradition stuck, and Black churches all over America still keep watch on New Year's Eve for the coming of an even greater freedom.

In Huntsville, the congregations of several churches gather for a joint service of preaching and music beginning around nine P.M. and ending around midnight. Each church sends a pastor to represent them. The assignment being to preach the gathered masses into a frenzy, each pastor has the job of outdoing the last. I had been given the ten P.M. slot, meaning that the pastors before me had already done their good work. I had heard the congregation shout and praise the Lord in word and song.

As my time came to preach, I prayed as fervently as my teenage heart would allow that God would make me into a proper Black preacher. But five minutes in, it was the same as it had always been. I couldn't quite capture the imagination of the people I loved, and they didn't understand me. The problem wasn't my voice. On the football field, my deep baritone had boomed with all the passion and drama of preachers like my grandfather and Pastor Montgomery. Nor was it that I didn't have confidence. You couldn't survive as a Black man in the South without a strong sense of self. But in the pulpit, I wanted to show another side of me, the part with sensitivity, the part that struggled.

With God, I'd learned, it was okay to be vulnerable. God had given me permission to soften my hard exterior and let the world know about my pain and my trials, in hopes that those who'd suffered might know that God waited for us on the other side. I had encountered God as a whisper or a mystery, and I longed to explore that. I needed to talk to him about the things I had seen and experienced. I needed to ask God in front of the world to help me make sense of Black suffering.

It took years for me to realize that I was not a Black preacher in the mode of my grandfather or the generations of Black men and women who preceded him. I had words to speak, but the primary place of their articulation would not be the rhetorical brilliance that is the Black pulpit. Essays were forming, but I did not yet know their contents. Books were struggling to get out, but they were obscured from me. The pastors could not see it; neither could I. In our context, those who chose God preached about God.

I came to understand that I had a calling of a different sort: to try to put into words and on paper the varied experiences of God in the souls of Black folks.

CHAPTER 10

Fools Fall in Love

I met the woman who would become my wife at the University of the South. When I began dating Mandy, I broke a rule that lingers in the background of most conversations about Black success. It makes appearances in our television shows, movies, rap songs, and comedy specials. The rule is this: Black men who escape poverty and make a life for themselves should date Black women. We should marry within our race. That is the rule, and I broke it.

As a kid, I used to watch interviews of Black athletes and movie stars. The host would ask them about the drive, focus, and talent that helped them make the journey from poverty to wealth. There would be clips of the athletes practicing and lifting weights, and then an inevitable shift toward their home life. But when the camera turned to the plush couch in the million-dollar home, the woman sitting beside the athlete was rarely chocolate. I remember looking at a white woman or a very fair-complexioned woman of color and then gazing down at my ebony tone, thinking that my favorite athlete or actor had sold out.

My future, I thought, would entail finding a Black single mother like the one who raised me. I would marry her, love her and her children, and bring them up as my own. I dreamed of forming a Black power couple that could inspire and encourage young Black boys and girls and show them what was possible. But I wasn't constructing a life; I was acting out a play. My fantasy emanated from a vain overestimation of my worth, a belief that I could undo the mistakes of my father by coming into a home, in a reversal of the way he'd abandoned mine.

It is wise and good to remind Black men in particular about the beauty and worth of Black women. It is healthy to lift up the Black family, that thing ripped apart by the slave ship and the master's whim, as a wonder to behold. I do not dispute the truth of that image.

What shall I say, then, to the people I disappoint? Life is wide and strange and wonderful, and stories are made by individual persons, not tropes. We move through the world, and if God is merciful, we fall in love. My marriage to Mandy is a manifestation of one of the many possibilities that occur when individuals are thrust together in school, church, or the workplace. I did not marry my wife to obtain some place in society that was denied me as a Black man. I married Mandy because—fool that I am—I fell in love.

. . .

There were no Black churches in the area, so when, in the second semester of my junior year, I went looking for a Christian community, I joined the largely white Baptist Student Union. It met in a classroom adjacent to the cafeteria, where my presence doubled the Black population in the room. Chris, one of my friends from the football team, had invited me to an earlier gathering, and I had turned him down with a flat no. But now here I was with that group, and in it I would find my future spouse.

More curious than nervous when I entered, I knew that white Baptists worshipped differently than Black ones, but I had little direct experience. The first time felt like a field trip of sorts. Instead of the organ, drums, and pianos that filled Black churches to the rafters with their sound, a single guitar provided the instrumentation for the gathering of two dozen students, who seemed intent on singing soft-rock songs to Jesus. Some of them put their arms in the air, hands straining upward as if God were only a fingertip away. In that way, they bumped up against some of the piety from my church back home. We knew how to worship God with our bodies as well.

During the talk that followed, the attendees fell silent. No one shouted back to the preacher or said, "Keep going!" They just sat quietly, listening. This preacher, like the students assembled before him, had less emotional range. If Black sermons were like a pot of water on a stovetop, beginning cool and working their way to a boil, these talks were a leisurely boat ride on a serene lake.

But the students were friendly. Afterward, two or three people approached me and said they were glad I was there.

They wanted to know how I had learned about them. I responded that one of the congregants was, like me, on the football team. He'd told me about them, and I'd decided to give their group a try.

They invited me to join them for dinner afterward in the "caf." I did, and one meal turned into two or three, until I was hanging out with them at least once a week.

They were earnest if awkward, speaking of a plan they had to evangelize the campus. When I asked them how we were going to do it, they responded, "We are going to bake some cookies and hand them out at the SPO."

"How are free cookies at the student post office going to convince someone to visit?" I asked, not understanding how a baked good would make someone think about Jesus.

"We are showing them the love of Christ in a practical way," they explained.

They gave out the cookies and added zero new members.

After I'd spent a few weeks with them, they figured out that soft rock wasn't my thing. One of them said, "I heard you like rap. Take this." He handed me a CD called *Jesus Freak* by a group named DC Talk. The group had two white guys and one Black guy in it. When I got home, I popped it into my CD player, only to be greeted by the same sort of Jesus rock music that played during their services. On a few tracks, one of the white members rapped a couple of bars, but this was not the hip-hop of Outkast, Tupac, Jay-Z, or Nas. His flow was fine so far as it went, harking back to an earlier era of hip-hop that used simpler rhyme schemes and less wordplay. But no one who knew the Black music scene would have recommended DC Talk.

For all our differences, though, we had one thing in common: these people loved God and were trying to honor him with their lives; I was trying to figure out how to do the same.

Mandy was a regular attendee of the Baptist Student Union. Both of us had moved around a lot as children. My family had traversed the neighborhoods of Northwest Huntsville, while hers had bounced around military bases all over the world because her father was a marine. Her family was Christian like mine, but she grew up in the charismatic tradition, a group known for its belief in miracles and speaking in tongues.

When Mandy reached high school age, her father exited the military, and she spent the rest of her teenage years in Columbia, South Carolina. She was an athletic girl who played soccer, but her real love was dancing. She did ballet, tap, jazz, and modern dance. She performed in both Christian and secular shows. She, too, had come to Sewanee on a scholarship, but not one rooted in financial aid. She was the valedictorian of her class, the epitome of the good Christian girl.

At Sewanee, she was reserved, focused, and quiet. Her frame was usually buried in the oversized jeans and baggy T-shirts that were the preserve of evangelical modesty culture, though later I would find out that the reason her clothes didn't fit well wasn't solely due to her conservative sensibilities. She was also shockingly cheap. Mandy had a job cleaning up the dorms at the end of every semester and would wear the clothes students left behind. "You can find some nice stuff in those rooms," she told me, citing, along with the outfits, a Game Boy she'd once found.

Mandy's good cheer and her delight in the small surprises ignored by others explained why anyone who spent time with her ended up liking her, even though they often couldn't quite articulate why.

Her faith was similarly upbeat. She attended Bible study every week because she loved Jesus. She liked to sing to him and wasn't concerned with much else besides her schoolwork and dance. I saw her from time to time at our Bible study meetings. Once, she came to our gathering fresh from a run, looking winded but happy, her brown hair curly with sweat on her forehead and at her temples. After the meeting, she wandered over to talk with a group of girls, and I was struck by how she smiled as she spoke. Her smile radiated from her whole self; it was in her eyes, cheeks, and posture, an expression of welcome that said, *There is kindness to be found here.* She glanced around the room and our eyes met, as often happens in an enclosed space with limited options. I saw in that smile not just some girl dressed in a T-shirt and shorts but someone I wanted to know. I wanted to make her smile like that at me. But the moment passed and I left.

After that, I began to mull over the idea of asking her out on a date, circling it like a car looking for a space in a packed lot. What did I actually know about her? She was Christian, smart, shyly beautiful, and kind. I found excuses to talk with her after Bible study and when I saw her around campus. She told me that she had only dated once. When I asked why the relationship hadn't worked out, she replied nonchalantly, "I didn't think he took his faith seriously enough." That statement stopped me in my tracks. I had been dumped for a variety of reasons over the years, but never for being too lackadaisical about my faith. With fresh insight into how to impress her, I pulled aside a few friends from the football team and told them that the next time they saw me chatting with Mandy in the cafeteria, they should come over and say something flattering about how religious I was.

The very next day, when Mandy and I were eating lunch together, one of my teammates came up and said, "Great job on the Bible study last week." Before he could turn away, another player approached us and said, "Hey, man, thanks for praying for me. It meant a lot."

I looked over at Mandy, who seemed surprised. Then a third guy approached us with a compliment about my piety. "I know what you are up to," she said after they'd left our table. "Nice try." Impressed, however, that I had remembered the reason she'd given for her failed relationship, she initiated our first date, which I think back on fondly as "the hike."

Having never voluntarily climbed anything in my life, I felt worn out by the steady pace with which she ascended the mountain and equally worried about taxing my legs. I had been trained for the starts and stops of a football game, not the uneven terrain of a steep slope or trying to match Mandy's relentless stride as she scrambled over hills and across streams. This was the Friday before we played our chief rival, Rhodes College, in Memphis. I spent the first part of the hike trailing Mandy, distracted by our coaches' caution to stay off our feet to make sure we were fresh for the game. "How much farther are we going to go?" I asked more than once.

When my feeble protests failed, I tried another approach:

"I've seen you around BSU a lot, but I don't know much about you. What's your major?"

"I'm biology and premed."

"Cool," I squeezed out between breaths. "What kind of doctor do you want to be?"

We stopped near a couple of large boulders, and I offered her a sip of water. That was when she told me that she wanted to be a pediatrician in sub-Saharan Africa. "Did you know that countries like Uganda only have around five hundred pediatricians for a country of over twenty-three million? And that America has around forty thousand?"

I did not know that.

"I have always felt called to be a medical missionary and help the poor," she said.

I heard her, but I was having difficulty processing the information. I was Christian and all, but my whole life had been about escaping poverty, and now she wanted to enter it willingly by becoming a missionary? I wanted to ask: *Don't you know what doctors make in the United States? You have the chance for a really nice life.*

She'd told me about her dreams, so I told her mine. Maybe I wanted to be as vulnerable as she was; on the other hand, I also knew that speaking would give me more time to rest. "When I came to Sewanee, I wanted to be a high school teacher and a football coach. It's why I majored in history. I wanted to teach history and help other young Black boys get out of my neighborhood and make it to college. But I'm starting to question that choice. I'm thinking about going to seminary instead."

That news did not excite her. She cocked her head in surprise and responded, "I never thought I would date a pastor. I know that some Christian girls dream of marrying a clergyperson and being a stay-at-home mom, but I've always wanted to work."

I found myself being honest with her, something about her sincerity working its way around my defenses. Once the break was over, we continued our trek, passing caves and gullies while continuing to talk. The date was a great start to our relationship, even though I played one of my worst games of the season the next day. Some things are more important than sports.

Things progressed from there. We spent a lot of time at the library and late-night food spots, our futures looming large in our conversations. I had received a scholarship offer early on to seminary, and Mandy began prepping for the MCAT and filling out medical school applications. While she tried to study, I tried to distract her, thinking that she took grades a bit too seriously. I would ask, "Do you really believe that one more hour of reviewing will be the difference between acceptance and denial at the school of your dreams? Will you look back on it all and say, 'If only I hadn't gone to get ice cream with Esau that Tuesday night, it would have all been different? Now look at me: I am unemployed and homeless!'" Often she would laugh and relent: "You're right. Let's go for a walk."

One night when I had convinced her to take yet another respite, I pointed up at the stars as we crossed the quad. "Do you see that?" I said. "That's the Big Dipper." Putting my arm around her to direct her vision, I added, "And that over there is Orion."

She glanced up in the sky and then back at me and said, with mock outrage, "No, it's not. Orion is not visible this time of year."

"Well," I replied, laughing, "I was only half paying attention in astronomy class."

Every Sunday she got up early to attend service at the university chapel, leaving the rest of the day for her schoolwork. I knew I was in love when I began dragging myself out of bed so that I could meet her there and we could share breakfast afterward.

During our senior year, we met each other's families. One would embrace us; the other would not.

The first time I took Mandy back to Huntsville, I told her, "You have to run the gauntlet. There are the church ladies, my aunties and uncles, and the teachers from Johnson. This is a bit of my world, and you ought to know it."

We visited during spring break, making the seventy-minute drive to Huntsville together. My mom was volunteering at the high school and had asked us to meet her there. As Mandy and I walked back into that all-Black space together, I was nervous. Would people think that I had gone to college and forgotten where I came from, because my girlfriend was white? At the administration office, they told me that my mother was in the cafeteria. So we went there. I found her having a conservation with the lunch lady who had served my food daily for the better part of four years.

When she saw Mandy, she said to my mom, "This that white girl you been telling me about? Well, don't be shy, girl, come on over so I can get a look at you." Mandy walked over, and the lunch lady continued: "Now turn around so I can see the whole of you."

Mandy glanced at me for assistance, and I just shrugged. So she spun around in front of the warmer for pizzas and Hot Pockets. The lunch lady said, "It looks like she has some good child-birthing hips. I think she will do."

My mother laughed, and Mandy turned a shade of red I had not seen before and have not since.

Our next stop was to meet the family at my grandparents' house. I didn't know what to expect, but my mom led the way. She introduced Mandy to a house filled with aunties, uncles, and cousins, which led to them flipping through old photo albums, my relatives pointing out pictures of me as a child. My grandmother Laura took a break from the kitchen to embarrass me. She told Mandy, "Anytime some little girl came around that took a liking to him, he would go to running, saying girls are gross." Then, with a twinkle in her eye and a knowing smile, she added, "I can tell by the way he looks at you that he ain't scared no more." Everyone laughed, and once again Mandy blushed.

When I felt confident that Mandy could handle the family on her own, I pulled my mom aside and asked, "Mom, what do you think?"

"She seems like a nice girl, very respectful. I can see why you like her."

"Mom, you know what I mean . . ."

"Oh, that she's white? Son, I have lived long enough to know that love is hard to come by. If she makes you happy, then be happy."

My shoulders, which had been tensed the entire time, finally relaxed. My mother was the most important person in my life. If she accepted us, I had reason to believe we would be all right.

When Mandy's family came to campus for graduation, I was, like any young man, nervous to meet the parents of the girl I was dating. Those few days were hectic, with both of us packing up our rooms, attending final parties, and saying goodbye to teachers and friends we'd made over the last four years, so at first I thought it was just a coincidence that her parents and I hadn't had a chance to meet. Mandy assured me that this was the case: "They're just touring campus." Or "They're at a luncheon." But as the days wore on, my fear increased.

Fool that I was, I decided to force the issue. I went to her dorm when I knew she would be there with them, and I knocked on her door. Mandy opened it, and I walked in. After I'd introduced myself, a silence fell over the room. My heart felt heavy, as if it might tumble down into my stomach. I knew what was coming next. Her father told me, "You seem like a nice young man, but I don't believe you are right for our daughter. We don't think society is ready for interracial relationships. We want to spare you all pain."

Instead of adrenaline surging through my body, I felt all of my strength leave me. Most of my life had been about facing obstacle after obstacle, and just once I'd wanted something to be easy. I was tired of fighting, more fatigued than angry. The rest of the conversation passed in a blur. I fled her dorm room, returned to mine, and went to sleep.

In the days that followed, Mandy and I would both receive our baccalaureate degrees, but we spoke little at the ceremony, apart from a passing greeting and congratulations. Her father's words would cast a shadow over the celebrations that followed.

Once her parents had left, she came by my dorm room. I could tell it was her by the gentle knock, but I did not know what I would encounter when I turned the knob. Getting dumped on graduation day was not an appealing prospect. I hesitated, but she plunged in before I'd gotten the door halfway open. "I'm so sorry, Esau. I had no idea they were going to do that. I was so shocked. I didn't know what to say."

The breath I didn't realize I had been holding escaped, and I embraced her—the lingering hug the only statement I felt comfortable making.

"So you really didn't see any of this coming?" I asked once we were sitting down. I felt shaken by what I might not know about her. I needed to hear for certain that it had been her parents avoiding me, rather than Mandy hoping to skip the confrontation.

"No, we have always been in diverse settings in the military, and our churches were always multiethnic. I'm still shocked. And so sorry."

Her response enabled me to voice the question that had filled my heart with fear: "Do you agree? Should we break up?"

"No, not at all. I love you. But for all their faults, I love my parents."

I wanted to tell her that I knew what it was like to love parents who wounded you deeply, but this was about her father, not mine. Instead, I replied, "I am more than happy to fail in this relationship, but I am not willing to avoid trying. I love you, too, and you are precious to me."

She smiled, and I couldn't help smiling back at her.

"Who knows," I said. "Maybe they will come around."

For a long time, they did not. Her parents and I would not speak again for years. Mandy felt the strain whenever they talked or got together. But rather than pulling us apart, their resistance clarified that what we had was worth fighting for. Mandy and I would begin to build something together, a few hesitant steps at a time.

Mandy had been accepted at Dartmouth Medical School and I into Gordon-Conwell Theological Seminary. Her campus in New Hampshire was two and a half hours north of mine in Massachusetts. Two southerners making their way in New England.

We both kept busy over the next two years. Mandy had a full roster of classes and labs, and I had the extra demands placed on me by classwork and service in a local church. Our relationship developed over the phone and during weekend visits. Mandy squeezed in calls to me when she wasn't cramming for an exam; I rang her when I wasn't trying to figure out ways to connect with a culture very different from the

South of my youth. She still dreamed of fighting malaria and AIDS in sub-Saharan Africa, while I spoke with her about finding justice here on this continent for the stepped-on peoples of my own country. We had no idea how these stories would fit together, so we let them bounce against each other as fall gave way to winter.

My proposal of marriage, which came two and a half years into graduate school, did not proceed according to a well-organized plan. Mandy had come into town for a visit, and I wanted to take her out to dinner. I went to the ATM, checked my balance, and saw that I had $62.17. In those days, paying in cash was still a common practice, so I took out my last $60 and hoped that she wouldn't order an appetizer or dessert. I believe that dinner was the first and last time I ordered a salad.

The meal ended up costing less than I'd expected, so I had enough money to suggest that we go to a coffee shop afterward. I knew that her final years of medical school would keep her busy; then she would have to complete her residency and her military commitment. Hoping to get an idea of when a wedding might fit into her schedule, I asked, "Mandy, how does your spring of next year look?"

"Why do ask?"

"I'm just curious about what you'll be up to."

"Spring should be pretty busy because I have a surgery rotation and then possibly internal medicine. I probably won't get much sleep then."

"What about early summer?"

"I think I'll be in Connecticut then."

"What about after you get back from Connecticut?"

"I should be in eastern New Hampshire doing a rotation at a rural hospital."

"Okay, what about next winter?"

"I think I'm going to San Diego."

Mandy could see that I was getting a little frustrated, but she didn't understand that I was trying to find a date that would allow us to plan a wedding. It seemed like she would always be busy.

I couldn't figure out how to ask her any more questions without giving away the plot. Luckily, she decided to grab a piece of the chocolate cake that had been tempting her all evening. She stood up from our table and walked over to the case that housed the dessert options.

In the time it took her to proceed to the cash register, make her purchase, and return, I decided to risk it all by proposing right then. But there was still a problem: I had no money and no ring. All I had was the cash left over from dinner, the coffee in front of me, and an ATM receipt for $2.17 in my pocket. *Esau,* I told myself, *use what you have!*

While she walked back with her chocolate cake, I gathered my courage. The chatter continued around us, but when she sat back down, my world fell silent, the two of us at a small, round table, two mugs of coffee and a piece of cake between us.

"Mandy, I don't have any money," I said. "All I have to my name is two dollars and seventeen cents. I don't even have a ring, but if you will marry me, I will spend the rest of my life loving you." I spoke without wavering, but as the words exited my mouth, my heart leapt to a fever pitch of beating against my chest. *What have I done? What will she say?* Hope and despair tussled within me.

I glanced up at her, expecting shock, but what I saw instead was a profound tenderness emanating from those green eyes. Without hesitation, she said, "Yes, I will marry you."

If my chest had thundered before, now her answer set off a nuclear explosion. I looked around at the patrons happily eating their desserts and sipping their coffee. How could they be so quiet when the world was brand-new and bursting with color? I turned back toward Mandy, unsure of what to do next. "Do you want me to drop to one knee?"

Mandy, the queen of decorum, said, "No, silly, we're in a coffee shop."

She would make me get on a knee later, after we'd bought the ring. Everything in its proper order. For now, she finished her cake and I smiled at the wonder of it all. We stepped out into the cold and quickly made our way to my car. Mandy called her best friend, Anna, and told her, "I'm engaged!" She recounted my foolish proposal, saying, "You know how Esau is. He does everything on the spur of the moment. He didn't even have a ring. I don't think he even planned to propose tonight."

That call was celebratory, and the ones that followed the next day to my mother and my siblings were equally happy. Then there was the call we were hesitant to make. We had to tell Mandy's parents. Over the next few weeks, it became clear that her parents would not attend the wedding, nor would they help pay for it. It is not easy to describe the toll this took on the woman I loved. I know how she longed to celebrate the beginning of a new life with me, her future husband, but each step—from shopping for a wedding dress to choosing the cardstock for the invitations—carried a bit of sadness. It tugged at my heart to see her joy weighed down.

My family didn't have any resources, and my meager salary as a youth minister hardly paid my own bills. But the church I served in New England stepped in to fill the void. Since our wedding would take place at the end of Advent, right before Christmas, the red poinsettias could be kept in place for the wedding. That red foliage, along with the wreaths and evergreens, would function as our floral arrangements. Without our requesting it, the church put a little extra effort into the decorating of the chapel that year, and the place was alive with color. In the absence of a catering budget, the ladies of the church volunteered to spend the afternoon in their kitchens preparing their best recipes.

Our reception would have the atmosphere of a potluck taken to the extreme, with cakes, finger foods, and winter vegetables lined with care along the back wall of the church's meeting hall. My mother had flown in a day early and made a German chocolate cake, my favorite dessert, for Mandy and me to cut during the reception. Local families had brought their fine china for the table settings. The memories of the congregation, their joys and sorrows, were there on each tabletop in the form of their treasured dishes.

It is customary in the pages of the New Testament for church members to refer to each other as "brother" and "sister," even without a blood relationship. The idea is that the church members form a family. Outside of the Black Baptist church of my youth, this idea had been largely notional. But as they prepped the reception hall that morning, I realized that this all-white New England congregation had become my family in truth. Mandy and I had new brothers and sisters, aunties and uncles.

My younger brother served as my best man. Getting dressed for the ceremony, he had some trouble with his tie. He is much taller than me, at a full six foot seven. As I reached up to help him, I thought, *Our father should be doing this. He should be here helping us.* So many lessons we had to teach ourselves, but here I was. I had made it. I had invited my father to the wedding, and he had promised to come. But as I walked to the front of the church and looked over the congregation, waiting for Mandy to enter, I saw that he had not arrived.

Mandy and I would share a mixture of joy and sadness at this seminal event in our lives. But whatever melancholy I felt disappeared when the music stopped and the congregation rose to their feet. The back door of the church opened, and in walked Mandy, wearing a dress that cleared my mind of anything else but her.

As hard as we'd worked to plan the other elements of the day—the food, the photos, the dancing—I had long seen our vows as the focal point. I do not know what promises my father made to my mother when they wed as teenagers. I only know that he did not keep them. Maybe as a result, the priest's words felt like a final challenge. I had struggled for a different life; now, standing on the precipice of one, was I ready for all it entailed?

"Esau, will you have this woman to be your wife; to live to-

gether in the covenant of marriage? Will you love her, comfort her, honor and keep her, in sickness and in health, and, forsaking all others, be faithful to her as long as you both shall live?"

I answered: "I *will*, with God's help."

Minutes later, I made the additional promise: "In the name of God, I, Esau, take you, Mandy, to be my wife, to have and to hold from this day forward, for better or worse, for richer or poorer, in sickness and in health, to love and to cherish until we are parted by death. This is my solemn vow."

I spoke those words with a conviction born of experience. I would not forsake her, and we had already had our share of "for worse." I trusted that God had something better in store for us.

A year and a half into our marriage, Mandy's parents asked her if we could meet. It had been four years since all of us had been in the same room. Instead of sitting down with them at the University of the South as seniors freshly in love, we met them at Dartmouth College as a married couple on the verge of Mandy beginning her military commitment.

The four of us gathered in our home, a small apartment near campus, the silence from the conversation four years earlier still lingering. Michael, her father, spoke first. True to the stereotype of military men, he is not given to long speeches or emotional outbursts. In terms of temperament, he and I could not be more different. But we had this in common: we both loved his daughter. He said, "We have had a lot of time to think and pray about the last few years. We also met with our pastor, who encouraged us to see that it was time to make amends. We are sorry for the hurt we caused you. We would like to have a relationship."

Mandy's mom, Judy, chimed in: "We can't undo the past, but we would like to try to have a better future."

Mandy looked at me. Even though they were her parents, she knew that I had to be the first to reply.

I had not known what to expect from this conversation. Their words surprised me, and at first I had no idea what to say. I took a moment to look around, my glance drifting from Mandy's parents to her, as I tried to settle in my mind who I was going to address. Was I explaining what I thought to her, or to her mother and father, or even, possibly, to myself? I'd spent years picturing a meeting like this, not knowing how it would come about.

I thought, *It took a while, but the church has done its work.* A pastor I had never met had intervened on my behalf and spurred my in-laws toward reconciliation. They had heeded his advice. But now that the moment was here, could I truly forgive?

The answer I returned to was what my faith has always taught me. Whatever other flaws they may have had, Mike and Judy had raised a wonderful daughter. They had instilled in her the values and character that had drawn me to her. More than that, I knew what it was like to live without a parent, the lasting pain of it. I wanted Mandy to be spared that experience.

People are always more than the bad decisions they make. As long as we draw breath, there is always a chance to start anew. That is the central teaching of Christianity. God gave us grace when we did not deserve it; that grace is a power that seeps out into every aspect of our lives. As the four of us sat in our little home in Vermont, I felt the power of forgiveness flow from me to them. I hadn't gotten the chance to repair the relationship with my father, but I could begin to restore this one. So I said, "A relationship sounds like a great idea." It was our first stumbling step toward healing.

That fall we had our first Thanksgiving with Mandy's side of the family. I knew her brother because he had attended the wedding, as had Mandy's uncle and aunt. The conversations were awkward and halting as we attempted to bridge four years of silence during a single meal. They didn't know me, and I didn't know them, but we were all trying. Although it would take years, we would succeed. We would become a family.

When I first met Mandy, she had the next decades of her life mapped out. To pay for medical school, she would join the navy. Her commitment would last at least seven years. Following that, she would take her medical talents to sub-Saharan Africa. I had dreamed of becoming a teacher and football coach and returning to Huntsville. Marriage is a collision of two people's dreams, dysfunctions, histories, and hopes. It always involves a form of letting go and making space. But out of those sacrifices, sometimes something glorious emerges.

We would never make it to Africa or to Huntsville. Life imposes demands that can upset even the best-laid plans. What emerged over the decades of our life together was something neither of us had envisioned. We would spend seven years with Mandy in active duty in the military, living in Chesapeake, Virginia; Okinawa, Japan; and Jacksonville, Florida. Following that, my burgeoning academic interests would take us to the University of St. Andrews, in Scotland, and then to Rochester, New York. We would have four beautiful kids together: Luke, Clare, Peter, and Miriam.

My marriage—and, more broadly, any interracial marriage—is not about racial reconciliation in America; that is too much weight for anyone to bear. We are not special; we are possible. Ours is like any marriage that lasts. We had to give up enough of ourselves to make room for the other person, but we had to retain a sufficient amount of who we were to avoid bitterness. All marriages become a third thing, neither one partner's dream nor the other's, but a different glory, an ordinary one we made together.

CHAPTER 11

Black Holidays

The most fun I've ever had playing basketball was a game against a bunch of drug dealers. Hollow Park was a contested space in my neighborhood. In the mornings, kids like me went there to play ball. In the evenings, teenage couples parked to drink and make out. Later, addicts arrived to inject needles into one of the few good veins they had left. When my friends and I made our way to the court as part of the first shift, those who played basketball in the morning, the activities that had taken place during the night were evident in the discarded beer cans, needles, and condom wrappers, physical reminders of different lives being lived in the same space.

I loved the Hollow Park court because it had chain basketball nets. The swish of a jump shot through metal has always reminded me of the noise made by the opening drawer of a cash register—a pleasant connotation for anyone who's dreamed of transforming their financial future through sports. Every spring a man would arrive in a white van, carry a ladder to the court, and put the chains on the rims that had lain bare over the winter. Within a few weeks, someone would steal them, and we'd have to wait until the next spring to have nets again.

But on this particular Saturday, the chain nets were still up. Corey, Brandon, Austin, and I were in middle school at the time and liked to play two-on-two. Brandon had the best handles. He could dribble circles around anyone. Corey had a killer jump shot. Austin was tall, lanky, and full of energy. I didn't add much to our collective skills, except for the distinction of being the only lefty. Most people are used to players faking left and going right. I did the opposite.

We were in the middle of a game of 21 when a car filled with much older males pulled up. A couple wore white tank tops, khaki pants, and Converse shoes, the basic starter outfit for anyone intent on intimidation. Others had on clothes fit for basketball: team jerseys or T-shirts and shorts. One of the jerseys had Dominique Wilkins's name on it, the other Penny Hardaway's, from the Orlando Magic. We felt angst in the pit of our stomachs at the potential for danger. Would they be the kind of men who ran us off the court? That had happened before, adult men announcing, "We running full court now. Y'all need to leave."

But this group was friendly. They walked casually, with a posture that bore no hostility. They didn't come to the court immediately, strolling first to the right of the blacktop to take off pagers and jewelry and deposit a cooler filled with forty-ounce bottles of beer. After setting up, they asked, "Y'all wanna run full with us?"

They split us up evenly, each team composed of two of us paired with three older guys for the first few games. As the day wore on and they made repeated visits to the cooler, returning increasingly inebriated, we asked if the four of us could play together. We did, and we beat them soundly, our youthful energy overcoming their size and levels of intoxication as they laughed, stumbled, and chased us around the basketball court.

I had fun that Saturday, but the good time came with a complication. I knew from the pagers, the jewelry, and the car they'd driven up in that these men sold the very drugs that turned my father into a monster. Later, I wondered how they could be kind to us on a Saturday morning, then leave the court to push the drugs that damaged our fathers, mothers, and friends.

I still do not know how to make sense of the combination of kindness and callousness in the same person. But, in truth, the possibility of goodness in those who do evil is not different in principle from the capability of good people to fail us. Things we separate intellectually into neat categories are messy in real life. My neighborhood, then, could be both dangerous and wonderful at the same time. That is why the idea of grace and forgiveness is so important to me. If we are all a mix of good and bad, then there is always a chance that the good might emerge victorious in the end, if we give God enough time to do his work. Patience with broken people and broken things is a manifestation of trust in God.

. . .

Recounting Black pain is uncomplicated and simple. The narrative arc is clear. The harder thing to explain is the joy and beauty of Black life in this country—complicated because these pleasures arise from the very same places and people who produce the trauma. Never is this combination of joy and pain seen more clearly than at Thanksgivings in poor Black spaces. Like church, all holidays are a "here comes everybody" experience; the promise of good eating brings the whole community together on neutral ground. The uncle on drugs, the cousin in the military, the nephew who's gone off to college, and the niece who dropped out— they're all there. Irrespective of the lives we're living beyond the dinner table, we are all one community when fixing a plate.

Every Thanksgiving during my childhood, we made our way to my Grandma Laura and Granddad Theodore's house to eat and laugh with people as varied as the shades of Black skin in attendance. At Thanksgiving, new dating relationships are announced and baby bumps are revealed. Even a couple whose marriage is in trouble puts on their best faces for their friends and neighbors.

The dress code? Show off your success. There is no better time to display the benefits of a new job (or hide the consequences of a lost one) than on Thanksgiving. I smiled at aunts and uncles in their best outfits, even if their suits looked like they would be more at home in the world of *Shaft* and other blaxploitation films than in 1990s Alabama.

The kids spent most of the day on the porch because the whole house smelled like chitterlings, the scent of boiling pig intestines overwhelming the aromas of pumpkin pie and turkey.

My mom's specialty was lemon meringue pie. I never cared for the meringue. Much to her displeasure, I would scoop off the fluffy top layer and head straight for the lemon tart. The pecan and coconut icing dripping from the sides of her German chocolate cake, still warm from the oven, defined Thanksgiving for me. When this cake appeared at my wedding, it was as if the whole of my childhood came alive in my taste buds to celebrate with Mandy and me.

When I was a kid, my mom told me the recipe was a family secret, its closely guarded ingredients passed down from generation to generation. So before our first Thanksgiving together, I asked Mandy to call my mother to ask for the secret to her recipe.

"There are no secret ingredients," my mother replied. "Everything you need is listed on the German chocolate wrapper. You can find it in any grocery store."

When Mandy told me this, I called my mother: "Why did you lie to me?"

"Things were so hard back then," she said. "I did whatever I could to make the holidays special, to add an element of mystery and joy."

My mom's deception was kind. Happiness is such a rare thing. She has always done what she can to expand it, to make it large enough for us to walk around in. I still believe that her German chocolate cake is special, available only to those blessed enough to be born into our family.

Everyone has their indulgences. One cousin fills his plate to the brim with nothing but meat and a generous helping of macaroni and cheese. An unspoken rule at Black Thanksgiving: do not take all the best sides. But he stacks his plate high without shame. Holidays are for eating whatever you want. No rules. Pretend you are not poor for a day. Laugh. Eat. Play spades. Share gossip.

The cousins closest to me in age were Coyle and Jerry, from my father's side of the family, and Michael, the baby of our group. Eight years younger, he would follow us around as we celebrated the holidays. All of us grew up playing together, taking turns spending the night at one another's homes. We were boys turned loose on the world, with only our mothers to rein us in.

The two miles between our home on Sandia Boulevard and theirs in the Meadow Hills formed a real divide. Where I saw addicts occasionally, they were exposed daily to a deluge of drugs and haphazard violence. As we got older, my visits to their homes became more and more rare. Soon our interactions were limited to my house or family gatherings, which meant that instead of happening every few weeks, our times together dwindled down to the holidays. In high school, we drifted apart. I got into football; Jerry, Coyle, and Michael dipped their toes first, and then their whole selves, into the alternative economies of impoverished communities. Only my brother and I would graduate.

But the bonds built during childhood run deep. I still hold close the memory of how we'd sit together on the living room floor at Thanksgiving (the couch and chairs being reserved for our elders), watching the football teams play. Even then, our conversations had an added weight, derived from the knowledge that after the meal, everyone would return to their divergent paths.

My last significant conversation with my cousin Jerry took place during my senior year of high school. After we filled our plates and ate, we sat down to watch all the NFL games. During a lull in the action, he asked me, "How is football going? You going to get a scholarship somewhere?"

I told him that probably I would, that there were a few colleges here and there sniffing around.

His question about my future gave me a chance to ask about his. "I heard that you dropped out of school. Have you considered a GED?"

He replied nonchalantly, "Nah, man, school ain't for me."

I pressed the matter: "Jerry, what *is* for you, then?"

He raised his voice, not shouting but displaying his fervent conclusion on the matter. "What do you want me to say, Daniel? There ain't much for a Black man to do but hustle. But I'm smart. I don't do nothing major. I sell to people I know and keep my head down. I'm good."

This drama had played out so many times—me trying to convince him to leave the game and him brushing off my concerns. We'd grown tired of it. Still, once it had begun, we had to see it to the end.

"I know that it's hard being a Black man in America," I said. "I'm Black right alongside you. But we can look around our neighborhood and at our own family and see what these drugs are doing to our people. We know how this version of the game ends. In jail or dead. Uncle Sam is undefeated. It's like that line from the Outkast song, 'The catch is you can get caught.'"

He was ready with his retort: "Everybody can't be like you and your sister. I can't play ball, and I'm not as smart as Tasha. Trust me, I ain't trying to flip burgers for minimum wage. But listen, everyone in the family is proud of you. Keep it up."

Jerry never did serious time for a drug offense, and in that sense he was right. Even so, a life of excess carries with it unexpected dangers. A little over a year after my father's death, Jerry and Coyle went to a club, as was their habit. They drank heavily, until neither of them was fit to drive. Nonetheless, they got into a car, and Coyle headed toward a liquor store, where they planned to pick up more alcohol to continue the night's festivities. On the way, he lost control of the car and hit a pole.

Jerry was killed instantly. Coyle went to jail on a combination of vehicular manslaughter and drug charges unrelated to the crash. Both of their lives ended, in different senses, in that moment. I got the phone call about their accident while I was attending an academic Bible conference in Denver. As scholars from all over the world debated the meaning of ancient religious texts, I struggled with guilt and the sense that I should have done more.

I had one male cousin left on my father's side of the family, and he died during the writing of this book. When Michael's mother passed, she left him a nest egg, as well as a home that had been paid for. The influx of cash made him popular. He threw parties where people who otherwise would have ignored him became hangers-on. Throughout much of his life, he'd struggled with diabetes. Without his mother to make sure he took his insulin and regulated his blood glucose levels, he lost his foot, then, later, the lower half of his leg. Whenever we connected over the phone or in person, he brushed off all of my concerns, always replying with "Don't worry, cuz. I'm good." But all of us who loved him were worried.

A COVID diagnosis was the final blow to his failing health. His body went into organ failure. With nothing more to be done, the hospital sent Michael into hospice care. When I heard that he was dying, I called him. "How you feeling?" I asked, not knowing what else to say.

He sounded terribly tired, his labored breathing apparent even over the phone. "I'm doing good, cuz," he said. "I'm going to be all right." One thing about Black men and our suffering: we have been trained to lie to each other. The other rule of Black male friendship: always accept the lie. But time was short. We had let too many lies stand.

"Michael, you are not doing good," I said. "You are on hospice care. The doctors are saying that you are going to die soon. You need to know that and to make your peace with God. You need to know that I love you, and that I'm sorry for what is happening to you."

Speaking about God on someone's deathbed felt like the worst kind of cliché, but just as I had, Michael had grown up in the church. My goal was not to frighten him but to provide some kind of hope, the idea that the resurrected life might be better than the one he had lived. By that time, however, he was too weak to say much else, and the conversation ended.

My mother went to see him the next day and recounted their last conversation: "We prayed, and I read him the Psalms. Then the nurses came in and asked him to sign a DNR form. He didn't know what it was, so I explained it to him. 'Do not resuscitate means that they are not to try and revive you . . . to allow you a natural death.'"

He seemed both shockingly innocent and a little confused, as if his impending death was a genuine surprise. His words came out in a whisper: "I never thought that I would go out like this."

My mom replied, "Nobody wants to die like this, but you are about to. Is there anything that you would like for me to tell people?"

Michael became serious now. "Tell them to take care of their bodies. Tell them I should have listened. The life with God would have been better."

My mother can be very sympathetic and tender, her voice capable of conveying an empathy developed during a life filled with its own hardships. "God loves you and will take care of you, Michael," she told him. "You're going to be all right."

I believe Michael's final words were sincere. At the last, God snatched the victory out of a life that looked so much like defeat. My cousin finally found some rest, a place to lay his head. Still, I would like to have seen his life filled with more joy than what he experienced.

Of the five of us, only my brother and I are still alive and out of jail. We speak about this often, the responsibility that comes from surviving, the deeply felt need to make sense of our cousins' lives and our own.

Michael, like Jerry, was so much more than a drug dealer who got his just deserts. He was a good-hearted kid, often unsure of himself, who spent most of his life looking for someone to accept him. I regret that I was so often too caught up in my own struggles to attend to his.

As for Jerry, I remember how he never failed to look me straight in the eye when I sat down with him. I knew I had his full attention. He made friends easily, and in a different world, he probably would have made a good living as a salesman. His options weren't as limited as he thought.

We are all responsible for the decisions we make. Jerry, Michael, and Coyle made their choices. But my cousins' struggles can't be understood apart from the circumstances that shaped them. In some ways, I see now that I was trying to hold back the tide with a chain-link fence. I could not travel back through time to our childhoods and ask the criminals to stay out of our neighborhoods. I could not go to the school boards and say, *Fund our elementary, middle, and high schools better so that my cousins won't fall through the gaps.* I lacked the ability to persuade the leaders of industry in Northwest Huntsville to stay put, so that our property values would not be destroyed. I couldn't stop the redlining or the policing that pressed down upon us until we broke under the pressure or left.

When I think about my cousins, then, I reflect not on our differences but on our similarities. How seemingly small decisions can blossom into life-changing outcomes. They got tired of being broke and decided to sell a little weed, and things progressed from there. That was not a decision unimaginable for me. I was talented enough to play football; they were not. Their mothers opted for cheaper rent-controlled housing; my mom felt it was better to squeak by somewhere else. Teachers took a liking to me and encouraged my intellectual development; they were treated like kids on their way out of school.

In more than thirty years of Thanksgivings, Christmases, and Fourths of July, I am not sure what my periodic interventions achieved. Black kids in my neighborhood didn't need to hear a speech at family gatherings. They needed a different set of circumstances, one in which hope was not so hard to come by. They needed a path through the wilderness to the promised land. But none of us knew the way. Instead we gave them turkey, collard greens, macaroni, and a game of dominoes a few times a year.

After I got married, my Thanksgivings hit the road. For several years, Mandy and I celebrated that most American of holidays in places as far-flung as Scotland and Japan. The stakes of those holiday meals were considerably lower. Gone were the young Black men debating and making existential decisions. Those conversations were replaced by small talk with middle-class expats: doctors, lawyers, and professors.

A man at one of these dinners once asked me, *What kind of traditions does your family have around the holidays? Are you turkey or ham people? Do the men in the family help or leave it to the women?*

I did not tell this person how I used the calm of Thanksgiving to try to convince my cousins to give up the drug trade. Or how I cannot remember having seen my mother and father both together and happy on any holiday. The mention of drugs, my single mother, or the people I spent the holidays with would feed into stereotypes about Black people. I did not want that. And what would this fellow have thought if I told the truth about how the only Black person in a room sometimes stops being a person, becoming instead Black people consolidated, a representative who must challenge Black tropes at every turn?

I did not answer the UNC moderator when she asked me to recount the worst incident of racism that I had ever experienced, and I did not answer the person who attempted a casual social exchange about holiday practices at home, because I did not trust them to hear part of the story apart from the whole of it.

Instead I asked my dinner companion, "Tell me what you all do." He was more than happy to take up the space I'd left in the conversation, and the moment passed.

My children do not eat as much on Thanksgiving as my siblings and I did years ago. The food is still a treat, but my kids are confident that when our feast is finished and the leftovers have been eaten, other meals of plenty will take its place. They do not need to stuff themselves. I float from room to room in the homes of middle-class folks and hear the latest conversations about a neighbor's recent promotion or plans to start a small business. Plans for vacation homes and summer camp drift in the atmosphere, replacing the smell of chitterlings that marked my childhood holidays.

My children's only visits to Northwest Huntsville have taken place during the holidays. They see me and my siblings when we have abundance and do not know how it contrasts with the deprivations of our childhood. They glimpse only part of my upbringing, the best part of it. But I realize now that I should tell them about the hard times, too, because there is no joy without suffering, and it is both the joy and the suffering that make me who I am.

CHAPTER 12

Fathers and Sons Revisited

For years, I thought my father hated me. The feeling began with our stalled road trip. Why else would you leave your child waiting like that and never bother to explain yourself? I see things differently now, with time having made room for extended reflection. I remember the excitement on his face when he thought of taking me with him. Somewhere along the way to get snacks for us, he must have let his fears get the best of him. The weight of fatherhood bore down on his faltering shoulders, and he had to escape. He ran. That was the story of much of his life. I can wish that he was stronger, but I cannot hate him for it.

I once feared that running was a genetic trait, and that I, too, would leave when my family needed me. So I built a life as the antithesis of my father's. We were to be two different people, as far apart as the East is from the West. But lives that are connected are not so easily separated. Every hug I give to my children and each sporting event I attend brings with it memories of my own youth. Am I doing these things because I care about my children, or am I trying to prove something to myself? Is it love or some mad experiment?

When my children were born, I thought my job was to be the perfect dad who always had the correct advice and could solve every problem. I had ambitions of being the husband who never forgot a holiday and often brought home flowers just because. I would never be selfish or distracted or unreliable. Years of parenting and marriage taught me that such perfection is beyond all of us. We fail those we love.

Looking back, I realize that I did not need a perfect father, only a good one. In hindsight, I can see that he sometimes reached for that goodness—a life with his wife and family—and in other moments raged against it. Whichever direction he chose, his family remained his center, the thing he strived toward or ran from. Every few years, he came back into our lives, promising that this time things would be different. I believe in the sincerity of those attempts. The look of joy on his face when he brought us Christmas presents was real. Coming home on payday during one of the seasons he lived with us, he handed my mom an envelope and said, "Laurie Ann, I haven't opened it; I brought it straight home." I could tell there had been a conversation about his checks and the fact that he often cashed them immediately to spend the money drinking or smoking. This time he hadn't done that.

A month later, he'd be back to delivering cash. I know because I saw the shame in his eyes when he lied about where the rest of the money had gone. By then, whatever drug had its hold on him had long ceased to be a source of joy. He was as much a prisoner of its effects as we were. But he never gave up. I came to see his lies and failures as attempts to be what he knew he should have been.

None of his returns during my childhood proved enduring, but a final return when I was well into adulthood gave me a glimpse of what might have been.

When Mandy and I got ready to buy our first house, we underwent a credit check and discovered that my score was shockingly poor, with over $15,000 in credit card purchases that I hadn't made. I reached out to the credit card companies to find out about the charges: a new cellphone line, pieces of furniture, a rental deposit, and various clothes, all purchased in the same part of Pennsylvania—which happened to be where my father was living at the time. I slowly understood what had happened: he had changed his name from Esau McCaulley to Esau *Daniel* McCaulley, so that he could use my identity to start a new life in a different state.

In the Bible, God chooses Jacob to become the founder of the nation of Israel. Jacob's older brother, Esau, is the unchosen—the one who, coming in hungry from the field, trades his inheritance for a bowl of stew. Instead of inheriting their father Isaac's property, Esau ends up becoming the father of the Edomites, the archenemies of the people of Israel.

Why would anyone name their child after such a tragic figure? According to family legend, my grandfather Gus had his mind set on giving his son a biblical name, but since he couldn't read, he let fate decide for him. Opening up the Bible at random, he pointed to a name, and that name was Esau. When my father told my mother that he wanted his firstborn son to bear his name, my mother resisted. She knew the story of Esau and Jacob. As a compromise, they added the middle name Daniel.

My father liked to call me Junior, a pet name I rejected. I'd say, "Dad, in order to be Junior, I have to have the exact same name as you. I do not. I am not a junior." Now, decades later, he had made it true by other means.

When I called the creditors to explain that I had not made those purchases, I assumed that if I told them my father had made them, my record would be wiped clean. This, in turn, led to a conversation with the legal authorities, who informed me that since this was a case of identity theft, and because I knew the culprit, I should file a formal complaint so that the issue could be taken care of.

The problem was that my father already had three felonies and was out on parole. About seven years earlier, he had been convicted of selling drugs to an undercover police officer. My father denied this, saying that he used drugs but never sold them. The difficulty was that he was so high at the time of the incident, he had no memory of the encounter. The judge took the word of the cop over that of the addict. Alabama had a three-strikes rule, so although most of my father's crimes were minor felonies related to theft, this drug charge was technically his third felony. The judged sentenced him to fifteen to twenty years, with no parole eligibility until he served at least eleven years.

Providence was with my father, however. Five years into his sentence, Alabama started a prisoner-release program. Since none of my father's crimes had been violent, he was let out early with the caveat that he not get into any more trouble. The terms also stipulated that he not leave the state, which meant that the identity-theft issue could lead to a parole violation, sending my father back to jail to serve the fifteen years remaining on his sentence.

"I can't do that to my dad," I told Mandy. "I can't be the one to send him to prison for the rest of his life."

"I understand," she said. We agreed to pay the bills and use my wife's credit as the foundation for our first home.

My immediate response had been anger. I thought, *Here I am trying to start my new life as a married man, and my past has come for me already. My father, ruining everything again.* I paced around the living room of the small apartment we were renting, trying to work out my excess energy. One way I calm myself down is by organizing things, focusing on small tasks that I can complete. I started to reorganize my books on our bookshelf, placing the books according to subject matter instead of alphabetically.

When the work was done, I felt composed enough to reconsider. My father had tried to start a new life by moving to a new city and changing his name. But his tendency to make mistakes had followed him. In much the same way, I could not escape my father simply by getting a few degrees and leaving the South. The consequences of how I was raised and the things I had seen would stay with me. This $15,000 was an example of that. Paying the debt was not about our relationship. It was $15,000 for a Black man's freedom, a bet that my father had a better chance of making a life for himself out of prison. That was worth the investment.

Years passed. I did not speak to my father about the decision to pay his bills. I phoned him when my son Luke was born, but he didn't return the call. I invited him to Luke's baptism, but he failed to show. We really didn't speak very much at all over the next half decade. My father settled into his life in Pennsylvania. He married a woman, but, like most of his relationships during this time, the marriage did not last. The drugs again became a point of contention. He found a truck-driving job for a company with lax testing procedures. Things carried on as they had always done.

Then, in 2012, my father went to the hospital complaining of pains in his chest. A quick scan of his heart revealed that three of his arteries were nearly fully blocked. He required immediate surgery. The doctors said that it was a miracle that he was still alive, given the extent of his blockage. They made it clear that if he continued his hard and rough lifestyle, it would kill him.

That particular brush with death stirred something in my father. He changed. Part of him must have known that such chances do not last forever. My mom tells me that he openly apologized to her for the abuse, in particular, saying that his memories of that time haunted him. He started returning my phone calls, and I answered his. He met my children for the first time when I was home seeing extended family.

When my sister Latasha got married, in 2014, my father was there. In the wedding photos he wears a black suit, a black-and-white shirt, and an ascot tie picked out by Tasha for the occasion. His hair has gone gray, a transition sped up by his heart surgery. Yet he looks healthy and happy—diminished, yes, but the charm my mother once fell in love with still resided within him. The only photos I have of him with my children come from that weekend. In my favorite, taken before the ceremony, my father is wearing a yellow polo shirt. Peter, less than a month old at the time, rides high in his arms. Closest to the camera are Luke and Clare alongside my sister Marketha's two sons, Jonathan and David. My dad holds Peter as if he's afraid he'll break him, the beginning of a smile on his face. The kids are all happy, and the sun shines in the background. Someone unaware of our family history wouldn't know the miracle contained in that moment.

After the photo was taken, I motioned for my father to come sit beside me. Over the last thirty years, we hadn't had many extended conversations. As the wedding planner showed everyone where to stand for the next photo and parents tried to keep their bored kids occupied, we talked.

I asked him the question that had been with me my whole life: "Why did you leave and why did you stay away?"

He did not seem surprised that I wanted to revisit the past, despite the festivities happening around us. He suddenly looked tired, the smile he had worn all day quickly fading. "Son, I don't rightly know. I do know that after I left, I saw that you were doing well, and I didn't want to mess things up for you. So I stayed away. But that doesn't mean that I wasn't proud of you, Junior."

I sat in silence for a moment, weighing those words against all the hurt and frustration that had piled up over all the years. I wanted a better answer, something that might undo the rush of anger I felt when I remembered the games and graduations and major events of my life that he'd missed. But some questions must be posed even if no adequate answers are possible. In the end, I decided to accept his answer for what it was: an attempt finally to begin a relationship. But because I didn't know how to say that, the silence stretched on.

"I'm back in church," he added, breaking the stalemate. "I've been attending this big church in Dallas called Oak Cliff Bible Fellowship."

My heart stopped. In college, when I was going through my own spiritual awakening, the sermons of Tony Evans, the senior pastor there, had given me a lifeline. If I could have chosen any church for my father to attend, it would have been that one.

But we were not used to displaying emotions around each other, so I played it cool. "Yes, Dad, I know that church, and I've heard good things about it."

"They got me in this Bible class," he said, "and they want me to write a paper. Son, I haven't written a paper in my life. Got any advice?"

Locating a yellow notepad, I outlined the structure of a standard five-paragraph essay. I'm not sure that I was making any sense. He didn't seem focused on what I was saying, his eyes often drifting to the rehearsal taking place in the next room. I decided to cut my impromptu lesson short.

Nonetheless, we were father and son, performing an odd inversion of the struggle with schoolwork.

The Bible tells the story of the prodigal son. One of two brothers asks for his inheritance early and leaves his family, only to waste the entire windfall on parties and wild living. This young man comes into himself while living among the pigs and returns home to be greeted with joy by his father. But in our family story, the children did not leave the father; the father left the children. He had missed my wedding and the wedding of my younger sister, Marketha, plus too many graduations, birthday parties, and holidays to count. None of that mattered to us now. He was here now for Latasha's wedding. Our prodigal father had finally come home.

It would be misleading to suggest that things were perfect after that. I had gone too long without a father. It wasn't a part of my rhythm to talk with him, and it wasn't his habit to call. On Father's Day, I would forget to send him a card. When we spoke on birthdays, we said, "I love you" not out of a sense of closeness but because that was what you said to each other. I never turned to him for advice, since I was accustomed to making decisions without him. He was in my life and I was in his, but it was a smashed-together thing, not a perfect fit.

I never spoke to him about the money, but I did mention that I had heard he'd changed his name. This became the source of a lighthearted ribbing: "Technically, I am Esau Daniel McCaulley, *Senior*," I told him. "You are a latecomer to the middle name. That makes you Esau Daniel McCaulley, *Junior*."

He laughed and said, "Shut up, Junior."

Another time, my mood turned serious. "Dad, I've thought most of my life about the name we share. I have never in my life met another person named Esau. In elementary school, kids used to make fun of me for it. They'd say,

'Esau, Esau, sitting on a seesaw.' The kids in church would ask why I was named after the loser in the Bible. For a long time, I believed that I was destined to ruin my future with some life-changing mistake, like the biblical Esau. I named my sons Luke and Peter because I wanted them to have normal biblical names. But I've read the story of Esau and Jacob over and over. Do you know what I've decided?"

He sounded interested, probably having pondered this mystery himself. "What's that, Junior?"

I told him that it was true, Esau did make a lot of mistakes. He sold his inheritance to his brother on a whim. But Jacob also took advantage of him. It was a cruel thing to do. In the story, Esau threatens to kill Jacob for his trickery, and Jacob flees. But when they are finally reunited after being apart for over a decade, Esau doesn't take revenge. He forgives his brother.

"Our namesake was not a failure," I said. "The biblical Esau was a complicated man who found his way to forgiveness in the end. He showed grace to someone who did not deserve it. It's too late now—Mandy and I are done having kids—but if I could do it over, I would name one of my sons Esau."

Never a man who displayed emotions, my father let me carry these kinds of conversations on my own. This one was no exception. He was quiet for a moment before saying, "Thank you, son."

After that, he moved the conversation to a more playful topic.

He came to see Mandy, me, and our children once while we were living in Rochester. It was the only time he got to meet our youngest daughter, Miriam. He said he had a load to drop off in Buffalo and would stop by on his way back. Unlike the hundreds of times he failed to keep a promise when I was young, he kept this one. I stood in the open doorway and watched that eighteen-wheeler come rumbling down the road and stop in front of our house. It was probably the only time a truck that big had parked in our neighborhood, other than when people were moving in or out.

The children rushed outside and gawked at the shiny silver semi with its huge wheels. He invited them to climb up to see where he slept and to play with the steering wheel. My oldest son, Luke, was enthralled by the same stories of travel that had captured my imagination at his age. It was all so ordinary. It took everything within me not to weep.

That was the last time I saw my father. He died a few months later, his heart giving out on the road that had claimed so much of his life.

My mother spoke to him about thirty minutes before the accident. He had called her, inspired by a woman he'd met at church. He had asked this woman out, but she'd turned him down, telling him, "Until you do right by your first wife, things are not going to go well for you."

My dad called my mom on the way back from dropping off the contents of his trailer in California. He told her what the woman had said. "She is right," he said. "I still miss you, Laurie Ann, and after this trip I'm going to come home and make things right. I still love you. I know that I've made a lot of mistakes. I've taken up over forty years of your life. I'm sorry. All I can do is pray."

My parents had been divorced for decades. His attempts at a reunion had become a part of the background noise of their lives, an impossibility that both of them accepted. But these attempts had taken on an increased earnestness after his heart attack. My mother was happy that he was doing better and had made it back to church, but she had no interest in restarting their relationship. Forgiveness is one thing; trusting someone enough to be vulnerable again is a whole different matter.

Laughing off my father's latest attempts at a reconciliation, she said, "Esau, I ain't got time for your foolishness right now. I'm with my sister Vanessa and we at the movies. It's about to start. I will call you later."

His heart stopped a little while later, his truck suddenly veering off the overpass and tumbling to the highway below, a single-vehicle accident.

I doubt that my father would have been successful in wooing my mother. But when I learned about that conversation, it cemented what I'd come to believe about him. He was trying to fix the things he had broken, and we all found it admirable, even if it was too late to shift the course his actions had set for us. It helped me see that for all his flaws, he never gave up. Even at the last, far from all those he loved, he was making amends, trying to find his way to the promised land.

My father did not live long enough for me to know him. Our declarations of love were always forced, something we knew we had to do. We never arrived at tenderness. But he did live long enough for me to understand him and, in so doing, finally understand myself. My mother helped make me who I am by her presence as an anchor in a troubled sea. My father shaped me through his failures and his striving toward something he never quite attained.

At the last, before he ran out of road, my father glimpsed the beauty of a life with God and his family. He saw, if only for a moment, a future in which he stopped running and made his way home.

A Funeral

The night my father died, I decided to put off telling my children until I figured out what to say. I tried to treat the following morning like any other. I went into the boys' and then the girls' bedrooms and said, "Time to wake up. Get dressed. We have church today." They moaned and stretched, but slowly began to rise from their slumber.

We are not a big breakfast family. We keep things simple: cereal and toast. Mandy stood in the kitchen making cinnamon toast. The children sat at the table next to the reading nook, chomping down on the Cheerios they called "purple" because of the color of the box. My daughter Clare, who was eight years old at the time, stared at me as if she could tell something was wrong. "Dad, are you all right?" she said.

Her innocent curiosity mixed with concern broke through my defenses, and I choked up. My children had never seen me cry. They rushed over instinctively to give me a hug. Luke and Clare led the way, but the younger two toddled along in their wake.

After a few moments, I composed myself and told them what had happened: "You know your grandfather that you met a few years ago at my sister's wedding? The one who came to visit us a couple of months ago? He died last night in California. We are all going to have to go to the funeral in Alabama. I will probably be the one who has to speak about him at the service. I will deliver what they call the eulogy."

After taking in this information, Luke had questions: "What will you say? What was he like? I did not know him very well, but he seemed nice."

"That is in part my fault, Luke. You should have known him. There is a lot about my family and my life that you don't know. My father is a part of it. But don't worry, as you all get older, I will tell you more and more. As for my father, he was a complicated man, and I will try to explain him in the sermon. I'm not ready to do that right now."

Clare, unsure of what else to say, said, "I love you, Dad."

I said, "I love you, too."

Ten days later we found ourselves at Union Hill Primitive Baptist Church, the place where I gave my first failure of a sermon and where Gus, my father's dad, had once served as a deacon. I hadn't spoken from this pulpit since graduating from college, my first halting attempts at preaching as a teenager a thing of the past. I was not a traditional Baptist pastor, but I had found my voice by preaching, teaching, and writing over the years, and as I took my seat with the clergy around the pulpit, I felt comfortable in my own skin.

Below us, in place of the communion table, a casket held the body of my father. Earlier, I had walked by and said my final goodbyes. Now my sisters and brother sat in the front row, next to Mandy and our children. Only Luke and Clare were old enough to understand what was happening. They looked terrified; since they had never been to a funeral before, this was the first dead body they had seen. Behind them sat friends, neighbors, and the rest of the extended family that had raised me.

It was heartening to see that aunts, uncles, cousins, teachers, and people from our various neighborhoods all showed to pay their final respects to my father. One by one, they all passed in front of his body. My mother went first. She paused for a second, placed her hand upon his, and then walked on. My sister Latasha came next. She stopped at the body and began to weep and moan. Unable to play the role of the stoic clergyperson, I left the pulpit area to comfort her. "It will be okay," I said, fighting back my own tears. "You have to go sit down." I would repeat those words to my younger sister, Marketha, when she stepped up. My brother, Brandon, paused at the body and moved on, not saying a word.

When my children's time came, I went to the end of their pew. "You do not have to go," I told Luke when he did not move.

"I want to go," he said, suddenly looking older than his nine years.

Clare chimed in: "Me, too." The two older children shuffled past the body with barely a second glance.

In the end, I spent more time in front of my father's body than I had planned on or expected. I was the last of my family to leave him. I wanted to say some final words to him, to have that last goodbye so common in the movies, but having missed that moment, I simply whispered, "I love you, Dad." I was glad to see the turmoil that had marked so much of his life now gone, replaced with an expression of peacefulness.

After a few songs and prayers, it was time for me to speak. I had feared that I might turn into a tearful mess, unable to articulate what I'd written. But as I stepped up to the pulpit, a sudden calm came over me. I opened my Bible, pulled out my manuscript, and began with a passage of scripture:

> "Two men went up to the temple to pray, one a Pharisee and the other a tax collector. The Pharisee, standing by himself, was praying thus, 'God, I thank you that I am not like other people: thieves, rogues, adulterers, or even like this tax collector. I fast twice a week; I give a tenth of all my income.' But the tax collector, standing far off, would not even look up to heaven, but was beating his breast and saying, 'God, be merciful to me, a sinner!'"

The Gospel of John records a conversation that Jesus had with Pilate in the days leading up to his death. During this conversation, Jesus tells Pilate, "I have come into the world to testify to the truth." Pilate responds by asking the most important of questions: "What is truth?" Stated differently, Pilate says that it is fine to speak about truth and falsehood, good and evil, but what does it matter in the face of your impending death? Does not the reality of death render all truth meaningless, leaving only the question of who has power?

Pilate's question to Jesus raises the question of the meaning of all our lives. My father is dead. Who was he? What did his life mean? Has death destroyed my father such that all that remains of him are the bits and pieces of a man that we can cobble together to keep out the darkness?

This is why the Resurrection of Jesus is important for Christians. The point is not that some man, by some odd twist of fate, defeated death. It is about the meaningfulness of life itself. Do our loves and losses and decisions matter, or are they all just a collection of events that end with our passing? Resurrection infuses our lives with meaning. It suggests that who and what we are echoes into eternity. Therefore, it matters who my father was, how he lived, how he died, and what hope we might have for him in the future.

In my early days of preaching, I spoke about my father as a good man who slowly became something else. I would usually omit certain parts, for lack of a way to talk about drugs. He became my testimony, in that I used to say to people that we are not defined by where we come from. We can be anything with the help of God. I survived, so you can, too.

As a child, I found it easy to hate him, but the older I got, the more I realized that people are complicated. Humans are more than one thing. My father was not just a villain; he was a victim. He hurt, in part, because others hurt him, especially his own father.

In a lot of ways, he was like the tax collector in the Bible passage on the previous page. The Israelites were an oppressed people ruled by a Roman emperor who did not love them. Nonetheless, the empire needed Israel's taxes to fund its further conquests. But instead of collecting the money themselves, the Roman officials hired cooperative Israelites to collect the taxes from their own people. These tax collectors were loathed because they joined forces with their oppressors and thrived off the misery of their fellow citizens.

The tax collector in Israel was a villain, but he was also a victim, oppressed by the Roman people. Tax collectors must have shared the same disappointment. They would have known the promise contained in Israel's cherished scriptures: that when the nation needed saving the most, God would rescue his people. But Israel had fought Rome and lost.

Having seen his people conquered and colonized, the tax collector must have wondered, *Is God not all-powerful? Or is God's power irrelevant?* Pushing down those questions, the tax collector did what he had to do to make a living. He got good at winning; still, he couldn't quite shake the images of the kids who went hungry because he had taken their families' earnings to satisfy his Roman masters, or the defeat in the eyes of husbands left emasculated in front of their wives and kids. He acted like his conscience was clear, but alone with his riches, he felt guilt. So he went to synagogue to contemplate his sad life and pray for God's forgiveness.

Like the tax collector, my father had his own return to God after his heart attack. In the last years of his life, he reconciled with and apologized to all of us. He tried as best he could to be a father to us. He left no inheritance, but he did succeed in one way where his own father had failed. My father's last words to his children were not the words of condemnation he'd received as a youth. He told all of us how proud he was of who each of us had become.

Christians like to believe that our faith is about people who convert and immediately change their lives. We envision flawless good citizens with well-mown lawns and perfectly behaved children. But life is hard. The road is long and winding, and the path to the promised land is not always clear. Nonetheless, hard lives are beautiful in their own way. Wanderings are instructive in their own right.

In the last years of his life, my dad took Bible classes, trying to break free of the demons that held him. He saw Jesus as a path forward. His journey is now complete. Sometimes our victory does not come through the glory of the lives that we live, but in the victory of Christ himself over death. God's ability to redeem broken things gives my father's life meaning.

The tax collector who went to synagogue could not bring himself to look up to heaven, but said, "God, be merciful to me, a sinner!" God forgave the tax collector and welcomed him into his family. My father told my mother, during that last conversation on the road in California, "All I can do is pray." He prayed, and I trust that God heard him.

Having fulfilled the task set to me, when I was done speaking, I nearly collapsed into my seat. For weeks I would mull over the sermon, thinking about what I could have or should have said, worried that I had not done my father justice.

Around Thanksgiving, I returned home from a conference and was met at the door by my oldest son, Luke. He was upset because some kids at his school had laughed at him. He said a teacher had caught him scribbling on a sheet of paper and asked what he was doing. He told her that he had planned to write letters to send to family members for Thanksgiving, and he'd realized that he couldn't send one to his grandfather because he was dead. Then he thought that if he wrote a letter, his grandfather would see it in heaven, because people see everything in heaven. The kids had laughed because writing a letter to be read in heaven seemed silly. I found it quite moving.

I asked if he'd been thinking about his grandfather a lot.

He had. I had, too.

Then he told me that when he got sad, he thought about my eulogy—how it was sad at the beginning, but the ending made him happy.

I told him that I understood. For a long time, all I could see were the sad parts. It took me a long time to see where God was in any of it. But I found him in my story, and the good news is that my father did, too.

Acknowledgments

Telling family stories that span generations is tricky. In some cases, many of the central figures in this book were long dead by the time I knew the right questions to ask. I often had to rely on the few surviving members of my family who could tell the tale. Black life among the poor in the South in the early 1920s did not leave much of a footprint to trace in official records.

For the events of my childhood, I had more assistance. My sisters, brother, and mother corrected many flaws in my recall. My younger sister, Marketha, the true family historian, was particularly helpful. She even visited the ruins of Wavon's house to take pictures and jog my memory. When the recollections of my siblings, mother, and I diverged, I had to trust my instincts. I hope that I got close to the truth of things. In a few places, I have intentionally changed names and locations to protect the privacy of certain individuals when it seemed wise.

To my children, Luke, Clare, Peter, and Miriam: These stories belong to you, and it will rest with you all to write the next chapters. Wherever you go, remember that God is a pillar of fire at night and a cloud by day. He will guide you.

To my wife, Mandy: No journey is ever too hard as long as you are there beside me.

To my siblings, Latasha, Marketha, and Brandon: I have not always been the best brother. I spent too much time in my own head, but I love you all dearly.

To all of my J. O. Johnson Jaguars and the rest of Northwest Huntsville: Cheers to us for never believing the lies or accepting the limits others placed on our abilities. We survived, made families, and built lives for ourselves. This is the Lord's doing, and it is marvelous in our eyes.

Special thanks to Derek Reed, Laurie Liss, Julie Shigekuni, and all the people of Penguin Random House and Convergent for all their help on this project.

Esau McCaulley is associate professor of New Testament at Wheaton College and theologian in residence at Progressive Baptist Church, a historically Black congregation in Chicago. He is the author of the award-winning book *Reading While Black* and the children's book *Josey Johnson's Hair and the Holy Spirit.* He is a contributing opinion writer for *The New York Times.* His writings have also appeared in *The Atlantic, The Washington Post,* and *Christianity Today.*

ABOUT THE TYPE

This book was set in Dante, a typeface designed by Giovanni Mardersteig (1892–1977). Conceived as a private type for the Officina Bodoni in Verona, Italy, Dante was originally cut only for hand composition by Charles Malin, the famous Parisian punch cutter, between 1946 and 1952. Its first use was in an edition of Boccaccio's *Trattatello in laude di Dante* that appeared in 1954. The Monotype Corporation's version of Dante followed in 1957. Though modeled on the Aldine type used for Pietro Cardinal Bembo's treatise *De Aetna* in 1495, Dante is a thoroughly modern interpretation of that venerable face.